Developments in ELT

General Editor: Christopher Brumfit

Approaches to Pronunciation Teaching

Editor:
ADAM BROWN

The British Council, Singapore

Modern English Publications in association with The British Council

© Modern English Publications and The British Council 1992
© Poems in Chapter 5: *Rhymes and Rhythm:* Michael Vaughan-Rees
© Chapter 6: *Sentence Stress – For More Meaningful Speech:* Brita Haycraft

First published 1992

Published by
MACMILLAN PUBLISHERS LIMITED
London and Basingstoke

Typeset by Wearset, Boldon, Tyne and Wear

Printed in China

A CIP catalogue record for this book is available from
the British Library

ISBN 0–333–58246–2

This issue is being published simultaneously as Volume 2, Number 2 of the
journal series 'Review of English Language Teaching'.

Contents

List of Abbreviations

CA	Contrastive Analysis
CCP	Consonant Correspondence Pattern (see Dickerson, chapter 9)
EFL	English as a Foreign Language
ESL	English as a Second Language
ELT	English Language Teaching
GA	General American
IATEFL	International Association of Teachers of English as a Foreign Language
IPA	International Phonetic Association/Alphabet
L1	First Language
L2	Second Language
NPKA	No Prior Knowledge Assumption (see Dickerson, chapter 9)
OHP	Overhead Projector
OHT	Overhead Transparency
PWSR	Prefix Weak Stress Rule (see Dickerson, chapter 9)
RP	Received Pronunciation
RSA	Royal Society of Arts
TEFL	Teaching English as a Foreign Language
TESL	Teaching English as a Second Language
TESOL	Teaching of English to Speakers of Other Languages
TP	Teaching Practice
VQP	Vowel Quality Pattern (see Dickerson, chapter 9)

Acknowledgements

The authors and publishers wish to thank the following who have kindly given permission for the use of copyright materials: Oxford University Press for the extract from *On the Move* by P. Buckley and L. Prodromou; and for Figure 2 in Chapter 11, reproduced from the *ELT Journal* 43; Longman Publishers for the extract from *Opening Strategies* by B. Abbs and I. Freebairn; and Cambridge University Press for Figures 1, 4 and 5 in Chapter 11.

The publishers have made every effort to trace the copyright holders, but if they have inadvertently overlooked any, they will be pleased to make the necessary arrangements at the first opportunity.

Chapter 1
Twenty Questions

Adam Brown
The British Council, Singapore

Introduction

It is my intention in this introductory chapter to do three things. Firstly, I wish to highlight what I consider to be important factors in pronunciation teaching. I have phrased these in terms of 20 questions. Trainers on preparatory TEFL/TESL courses might like to use these as the starting point for discussions on the nature of pronunciation teaching and its role within ELT.

Secondly, I have included a reasonably large References section. This, in conjunction with the References sections of the other chapters, should provide an adequate springboard for the interested reader to delve more deeply into the subject of pronunciation teaching. The References section and the 20 questions together do not in themselves provide an exhaustive coverage of the field. For example, the topic of pronunciation learning (as opposed to teaching) is barely touched on in the present collection. Other articles describing the state of the art have appeared elsewhere (e.g. Leather, 1983; Morley *et al.*, 1975; Pennington and Richards, 1986; von Schon, 1987) and the reader is recommended to consult these for a fuller picture of the subject. A useful bibliography of books and articles on pronunciation teaching appears in Brown (ed. 1991:359–370). Several books are available covering the whole field, for example, Haycraft (1971), Kenworthy (1987), MacCarthy (1978), Tench (1981).

The third purpose of this chapter is as an introduction to the other contributions to the present collection.

1 What's wrong with RP?

A crucial question, before determining *how* to teach pronunciation, is to establish *what* to teach. In other words, what is the pronunciation target which we hope students will eventually achieve? In the past, textbooks published in Britain have almost exclusively used the accent known as Received Pronunciation (RP). Although the use of RP as a worldwide pronunciation model has come under much criticism, the practice still continues.

There are few advantages to using RP as the model. The main one is that it is a well-described accent and materials are readily available which use RP. However, this is a *de facto* situation: RP materials exist and therefore teachers use them. Instead, a logical sequence would dictate that teachers should decide whether RP is the accent to be used. If so, then RP materials may be used; if not, then materials should be written using whatever alternative accent is chosen.

It has often been stated that RP is a widely understood accent. This is admittedly true; however, so is the fact that many other accents of English are equally intelligible throughout the world. In particular, the US accent known as General American (GA) is familiar to most people, owing to the influence of American culture. This is manifest in the pervasive nature of US films, TV programmes and business. We must also remember that there are over 250 million US citizens, many of whom travel widely on business and holiday. Other standard native accents are therefore equally suitable as pronunciation models. In any case, it is often doubtful whether learners can reliably distinguish different accents of English.

It has been argued in the past that RP is a regionless accent; it was not possible to tell which part of Britain a speaker came from, if he or she spoke RP. This was given as an argument for the adoption of RP as an accent representative of most of Britain. Nowadays, however, RP is associated (in the minds of British people if not in statistical reality) with England, and especially the south-east of England (London and the Home Counties). This has weakened this argument for RP as a pronunciation model.

In contrast to the weak arguments for RP, there are several strong arguments against it. It is important to realise just how few speakers of RP there are. Even generous estimates put the figure at less than 5 million worldwide. This has two important implications. Firstly, the likelihood of a learner ever talking to an RP speaker is small. Secondly, the number of English language teachers with RP accents is also small, and thus there is a discrepancy between what learners hear from their teacher and what they are presented with in pronunciation materials such as books and tapes.

It must be remembered that language is essentially a social pheno-menon, and it thereby helps us to convey our social identity as much as other aspects of behaviour such as dress. Many learners have no intention of mastering an RP accent (or at least have no intention of using one outside the classroom), since they have no reason to wish to identify themselves with the native RP-speaking community.

The prestige of RP has declined dramatically over the last few decades. In the earlier part of the century, it carried prestige because of its association with the British 'public' (i.e. private fee-paying) schools, and the fact that such RP speakers usually went on to careers in government, the legal profession, or some other senior professional post. At one time it was a prerequisite for BBC announcers, whereas nowadays even quite strong regional accents are heard. The prestige has been lost and an RP accent may nowadays lead to stigmatisation and even vilification.

A final disadvantage for RP is that, from the phonetic point of view, it is not a particularly easy accent of English to master. GA is easier in many respects. The phonetician David Abercrombie has long argued that Scottish English is phonetically easier, and would make a more suitable pronunciation model on other counts too.

To sum up then, there are stronger arguments nowadays against RP as a pronunciation model than for it. These have been summarised by Macauley (1988) in his article 'RP R.I.P.', in which he suggests that it is time that the death knell were tolled for RP as a pronunciation model.

2   In pronunciation teaching, is there a difference between ESL and EFL?

The distinction between ESL and EFL has been used in talking about the status of English in non-native situations (Moag, 1982). It is essentially a socio-linguistic distinction. In ESL situations, English has official status, is used widely in government, the media and education, and is in widespread use in the everyday life of the people. In contrast, English in EFL situations has low official recognition and is used mainly for communication with foreigners rather than with locals. In ESL situations, a local form of English has traditionally been accepted as the educational model, whereas in EFL situations, a native model has been used.

The distinction is, however, rather shaky. Several countries, such as India, Malaysia, the Philippines, Sri Lanka and Tanzania, are in transition from ESL to EFL, and some writers (Hill, 1982) have argued that certain countries do not fit well into either category. Indeed, some countries (for example, Singapore) hover between second-language and native-language status.

As far as pronunciation models are concerned, the factors arguing for a local model for ESL situations generally apply equally to EFL situations (Brown, 1989). Consequently, the ESL/EFL distinction does not seem a particularly useful one in pronunciation teaching.

3   How important is intelligibility?

Language is a system by which people can communicate with each other. Very often this communication takes the form of the speaker transferring information, ideas and attitudes to the listener, although it has other social functions. If intelligibility means the success with which a speaker conveys his message to the listener, then it is obviously a very important factor in pronunciation teaching as in all other aspects of ELT.

So far, I doubt whether many readers would take great exception to the above argument. Intelligibility is important. Problems arise when we start considering exactly what intelligibility is, and how it is achieved. It often seems that intelligibility depends as much on the listener and the context, as it does on the speaker's pronunciation. For example, if a stranger stops you in the street and asks you something, there is a great possibility of your not understanding him at first hearing. This is unlikely, however, if you have been holding a conversation with someone for 10 minutes. The stranger might ask you almost anything (the way to somewhere, if you speak French, if you have the time, etc.), whereas the possibilities for the next utterance in a 10-minute conversation are severely limited by what has been said in the previous utterances. After chatting to someone for 10 minutes, you have had time to 'tune in' to his accent, whereas a total stranger's accent poses problems in this respect.

Given that intelligibility is essentially interactional in nature, Smith and Nelson (1985) suggest that the terminology used in this area should be made more precise. They propose that *intelligibility* be restricted to the low-level oral/aural recognition of words and utterances; *comprehensibility* can then be used for the understanding of the meaning of words or utterances (the locutionary force, in speech act terms); finally *interpretability* refers to the understanding of the meaning behind words or utterances (the illocutionary force). They claim that problems of miscommunication arise more often in terms of comprehensibility and interpretability, than of intelligibility.

However one defines it, intelligibility is clearly important, although work still needs to be done on exactly what it is and how it is achieved.

4   Is clarity a useful concept?

The term *clarity* is also used sometimes in discussions on pronunciation teaching, but again it is not a well-defined term. Two different senses can be distinguished. In the first, the term is synonymous with intelligibility (in fact, interpretability in Smith and Nelson's terms). Thus, often when we say 'Do I make myself clear?', we mean 'Do you understand me?'.

Alternatively, the term may be used to refer to pronunciation. In this sense, it refers to the care with which sounds are articulated. This may not, however, be a desirable goal in pronunciation teaching. For example, Temperley (1983, 1987) has shown that most native speakers regularly omit (*elide*) the /t, d/ in words such as *tents*, *acts* and *bands*, such that they are identical in pronunciation to *tense*, *axe* and *bans*. The reason for this is simple: these words are easier to pronounce without the /t, d/. Obviously intelligibility is not seriously affected, otherwise native speakers would not run the risk of being misunderstood and would stop omitting these sounds. Therefore, Temperley argues, there is little justification for English language teachers to insist that learners pronounce these /t, d/s. Even though the pronounciation is less clear and less deliberate, it is more natural and no less intelligible. In this sense then, clarity does not seem a useful concept.

5 Is listening comprehension a part of pronunciation teaching?

Listening comprehension naturally goes hand-in-hand with pronunciation as the perceptive and productive processes respectively of the spoken medium of language. Listening comprehension may therefore be usefully included in programmes of pronunciation teaching, and vice versa, as there are spin-offs in both directions. Some courses (e.g. Gilbert, 1984; Rogerson and Gilbert, 1990) include both.

One instance where the influence of pronunciation on listening comprehension is evident is the process of simplification. As Temperley notes, there is no need for teachers to insist that students meticulously enunciate all the consonants in certain clusters, since native speakers regularly simplify these combinations. In view of this, however, it is necessary that students are given practice in listening to such natural simplified speech.

Listening comprehension is improved for the learner if he is made aware of processes of simplification such as elision (omission of sounds) and assimilation (change of sounds). Whether he introduces these features into his speech or not, though, should be left as a consequence of his developing fluency in English.

Another important function of listening comprehension is the familiarisation of learners with a wide range of accents of English. This is necessary to ensure comprehension in real life situations outside the classroom. It also helps to make the learner aware that substantial variation in pronunciation is possible while still retaining a high level of intelligibility.

6 How do students feel about pronunciation?

As was mentioned above, language (including pronunciation) is a social phenomenon, and the attitudes, needs and desires of learners therefore play a role in the success of ELT.

Shaw (1981) used a questionnaire to investigate the attitudes of 170 Singaporean, 342 Indian and 313 Thai students. The following data compared their attitudes to the four skills: reading, writing, listening and speaking. *Speaking* here includes oral fluency as well as pronunciation.

	Singapore	India	Thailand
1 Speaking is my worst skill	47%	59%	62%
2 I want speaking to be my best skill	71%	71%	88%

Clearly, students attach great importance to speaking but, as Shaw (1981:116) concludes, 'there is a great difference between what the students want and what they are getting from their English classes'.

Classroom time may be usefully devoted in the initial stages to discussion of students' attitudes towards ELT, and pronunciation in particular. Kenworthy (1987:55) suggests that questions such as the following may be discussed (in the students' native language, if necessary) in order to emphasise the importance of 'good pronunciation'.

1   Imagine you are talking in your own language with a foreigner. The person doesn't speak your language very well and is very difficult to understand. What do you do?
2   What do you say when the foreign speaker apologises for his poor accent?
3   How do you feel when a foreigner pronounces your name wrong?
4   How do you feel when you meet a foreigner who speaks your language with a very good accent?

Similar preparatory exercises are given by Ellis and Sinclair (1989) for 'learner training' in other aspects of ELT.

7   Do teachers need a knowledge of phonetics?

Abercrombie (1956:28) writes:

It is not possible, for practical purposes, to teach a foreign language to any type of learner, for any purpose, by any method, without giving *some* attention to pronunciation. And any attention to pronunciation *is* phonetics.

We might want to disagree with the all-embracing nature of the above statement. There are ELT students who require English only, or predominantly, in order to read and write business correspondence or scientific articles. For these students, pronunciation may not be a prime concern. But by and large, pronunciation surfaces in most ELT courses. To the above questions, then, we may respond with a firm 'yes'.

Two related questions are less easy to answer. Given that teachers need a knowledge of phonetics, we might ask whether most English language teachers at present possess an adequate knowledge of phonetics. A grounding in phonetics is clearly required in preparatory TEFL courses. Ross (chapter 2 in this collection) offers a syllabus for integrating 'phon. and pron.' training into such courses.

We might also ask whether phonetic description needs to appear in ELT classes. We need phonetic knowledge to understand how problem sounds such as /θ/ as in *thin* are produced. /θ/ is phonetically known as a voiceless dental fricative, which means that air escapes with a hissing noise between the gap left between the tip of the tongue and (the back face of) the upper teeth; the vocal cords do not vibrate. However, knowledge of a more pedagogical nature is also required, in order to convert this information into effective classroom teaching strategies, for example, for distinguishing /θ/ from /t/ (a voiceless alveolar stop) as in *tin*. The main difference lies not in the place of articulation (/θ/ is dental, while /t/ is alveolar for most speakers), but in the manner of articulation. /θ/ is a *continuant* sound, which means that air escapes throughout its production, whereas /t/ is non-continuant or *obstruent* – air does not escape and the sound is time-bound. You can therefore prolong a /θ/ but not a /t/.

Do teachers need to use phonetic description in class? Do they need to use and explain terms like *dental, fricative, stop* and *continuant*? The answer depends largely on the particular group of learners being taught. Some learners will achieve an accurate /θ/ simply by imitating the sound produced by the teacher. Others will benefit from a more intellectualised approach, using a phonetic description, perhaps even a head diagram (see my other contribution to this collection, chapter 11). Strevens (1974) refers to these as the principles of innocence and sophistication respectively. As a broad generalisation, imitation is more successful with younger learners, while older learners appreciate the more descriptive approach.

Phonetics therefore need not surface in the classroom, although a knowledge of phonetics is necessary for teachers. Many introductory books on phonetics exist; personal favourites are Knowles (1987), Ladefoged (1982), Roach (1983) and Wells and Colson (1971).

8   Do teachers need a knowledge of phonology?

The distinction between phonetics and phonology may not be clear to the reader. Phonetics deals with the description of speech sounds – how they are produced by the vocal apparatus. Phonology deals with the way that speech sounds work together in the sound system of a language. In short, phonetics deals with form, phonology with function. Phonetics may be language-independent, whereas phonology must refer to a particular language. The two are not totally separate; it is impossible (or at least unwise) to do phonetics without keeping an eye on phonology, and vice versa. It should also be pointed out that in Britain the word *phonetics* is often used in a wider sense subsuming phonology, and in the USA the word *phonology* is often used more widely subsuming phonetics.

It is therefore a matter of phonetics to say that /θ/ is a voiceless dental fricative. However, it is a phonological statement to say that /θ/ can only combine with /r/ (as in *three*) in syllable-initial position in English. /θj-/ and /θw-/ are also possible, but occur in very few words, such as *enthusiasm*, or *thwart*. Phonology therefore tells us that /θr-/ needs to be practised if /θ/ is a problem, so that *three* is distinct from *tree*. Phonology is thus useful to the English language teacher, in certain areas such as clusters, but probably less so than a sound foundation in phonetics.

9   How useful is phonetic transcription?

For many people, phonetics is thought of as synonymous with phonetic transcription, the process of using phonetic symbols. Phonetic symbols are obviously important in phonetics, but they are only tools of the trade, and are of little use without a knowledge of the phonetic information on which they are based.

> The use of phonetic symbols is a very valuable part of the phonetician's technique, but it is perfectly possible to teach pronunciation without making use of them, and it is also possible, and alas! quite common, to use phonetic symbols without succeeding in teaching pronunciation. (Abercrombie, 1956:29)

There are, however, two respects in which phonetic symbols are of great use in ELT. The first concerns the use of dictionaries for finding out the pronunciation of an unfamiliar word. All good modern learners' dictionaries use phonetic symbols to indicate pronunciation, and learners must therefore be familiar with them. This does not necessarily mean that they should learn them by heart. In any case, learners' dictionaries provide a key to these symbols for easy reference, usually in some convenient place such as an inside cover.

Secondly, there is one sound in English which is very difficult to refer to, and therefore a phonetic symbol may help. It is the so-called *schwa*, as in the first and last syllables of the word *procedure*. It is, in some ways, the most important vowel in English:

(i)   It is the commonest English vowel; roughly 25 per cent of all vowels in connected spoken English are *schwa*.
(ii) Most unstressed syllables contain this vowel; it is therefore a very basic feature of the English stress system.
(iii) Failure to use this vowel properly often marks a person's speech as 'foreign'.

The problem is that there is no spelling which consistently represents *schwa*. As Upward (1988:24) notes, it may be represented by a wide range of vocalic spellings: compare *burglar, teacher, amateur, Cheshire, doctor, vigour, centre, murmur, injure, martyr*. It is therefore very useful for learners to know the phonetic symbol for *schwa*; it is an inverted *e* – /ə/.

Tench (chapter 8) outlines a number of exercises in which a knowledge of the phonetic alphabet is useful for ELT students.

10   Is English spelling as chaotic as it sometimes seems?

The English spelling system has often been described as chaotic and unreliable for purposes such as teaching. Critics of the system cite examples where the correspondence between written letters and spoken sounds is far from one-to-one. For instance, in the series *cough*, *bough, through, enough, thought, although* and *thorough*, the same *ough* spelling represents seven different sounds (or sound combinations).

However, such critics generally overlook the many other examples where English spelling is very regular. In Hanna *et al.*'s (1971) study, it was found that 84 per cent of English words were completely regular, whereas only 3 per cent were so irregular that they would need to be learnt by rote (like the *ough* examples). If English spelling were truly chaotic, then attempts at spelling reform would have met with greater success than they have.

There therefore seems little problem in teachers using spelling or a spelling-based system, rather than phonetic symbols, to refer to most sounds, especially consonants. This is a point made by Dickerson (chapter 9), who also shows how spelling provides reliable clues at all levels of pronunciation.

11   How useful is phonological contrastive analysis?

Contrastive analysis (CA) may be applied at all levels of language – phonology, grammar and vocabulary. James (1980:3) provides the following definition:

> CA is a linguistic enterprise aimed at producing inverted (i.e. contrastive, not comparative) two-valued typologies (a CA is always concerned with a *pair* of languages), and founded on the assumption that languages can be compared.

CA thus describes the systems (for present purposes, the phonological systems) of two languages, with the assumption that significant differences between systems will constitute major problems for the language learner, and should therefore be a major focus of attention for the language teacher and syllabus writer.

James (1980) proposes four steps in a phonological CA:

1   Inventorise the phonemes of L1. That is, list the phonemes of the learners' L1, for example in tabular form in consonant and vowel charts. For most languages of the world, such inventories have already been prepared by phonologists.
2   Inventorise the phonemes of L2.
3   State the allophones of each phoneme of L1 and L2. That is, list the non-distinctive phonetic segments of each language.
4   State the distributional restrictions on the allophones and phonemes of L1 and L2. Steps 3 and 4 are really two sides of the same coin, since any allocation of allophones to phonemes must be done on the basis of distributional criteria.

Such a CA may then be used for predicting learners' difficulties in mastering the L2 phonology. We may distinguish four broad categories of difficulty:

1   Sounds which L1 has, but which L2 does not have. These sounds are, by and large, irrelevant for language teaching.
2   Sounds which both L1 and L2 have, and which are used in similar ways in the two phonological systems. These sounds are relevant, but should pose no real problems.
3   Sounds which both L1 and L2 have, but which are used in different ways in the two languages. Although learners should have no difficulty in pronouncing the sounds *per se*, they may encounter some difficulty in remembering to use the right sounds in the right phonological contexts.
4   Sounds which L2 has, but which L1 does not have. These sounds are therefore 'new' sounds whose pronunciation needs to be learnt, both in isolation and in phonological contexts in words and sentences. They may therefore be very difficult.

Certain writers have devoted pages to lists of 'problem sounds' of the third and fourth types above for learners of English as the L2, for example, Swan and Smith (1987), and Haycraft (1971) for learners with European L1s. These lists certainly identify the main difficulties in English pronunciation for foreign learners, although they often seem the result of *post hoc* description rather than of predictive CA.

12   How can we decide which aspects of pronunciation are important?

Some writers add a fifth step to the four outlined above for CA. This step relates to statistical information concerning the use and distribution of phonemes. It has two parts:

1   A statement of the frequency of phonemes in connected text.
2   A statement of the frequency of phonemic contrasts in words of each language.

The two parts fall under the label *functional load*. It is possible to have two languages with identical phonemic inventories, but in which the corresponding phonemes and contrasts are used to differing degrees in connected text and in the lexicon of each language (Herdan, 1958), that is, they have different functional loads. Elsewhere (Brown, 1988, 1991) I have shown, for example, that the English /e, æ/ contrast is very important; both phonemes occur frequently, are distinct in all native accents of English, and give rise to numerous minimal pairs. In contrast, /u:, ʊ/ are both infrequent phonemes, are conflated by many Scottish speakers, and produce few minimal pairs; it may therefore be considered an unimportant contrast and may be given less priority in pronunciation teaching materials. In the above works I include a rough-and-ready ranking of the overall importance of those English phonemic contrasts often conflated by foreign learners.

The overall importance of intelligibility (as opposed to a quasi-native accent) as a criterion is again emphasised, by Kenworthy (1987), who gives lists of problem sounds for several L1 groups of learners. However, some attempt at prioritisation is made, by labelling features *high priority*, *low priority* or *optional attention*.

> Some problems learners have need to be given *high priority* because they are vital for intelligibility; others do not affect intelligibility and can be given *low priority* ... Learners may also have problems which can be given *optional attention*. These are features which, although they may contribute to a very noticeable foreign accent, will not usually lead to intelligibility problems. (Kenworthy, 1987:123)

13 Which are more important – segmentals or suprasegmentals?

All the discussion so far on CA has been at the level of consonants and vowels, so-called segmental phonology. James (1980:80) claims that 'of equal or greater important is CA of the suprasegmental phenomena: the features of stress/rhythm and intonation in particular'. However, he does not elaborate on suprasegmental CA at all, and very little has been done in this respect. The 'building block' nature of consonant and vowel segments makes comparison and contrast attractive whereas suprasegmental features are generally of a far less conducive nature.

Most modern writers, though, are agreed that suprasegmental features are, if anything, more important than segmental in terms of intelligibility and the acquiring of a quasi-native accent. Kenworthy (1987:123) notes that 'in general, the areas of rhythm, word stress, and sentence stress are *high priority* areas for *all learners*'.

In terms of the interactional nature of speech, emphasised above, Mehrabian and Ferris (1967) have quoted the following figures for the weight of importance in communication: face, 55 per cent; tone, 38 per cent; words, 7 per cent. Segmental consonant and vowel pronunciation relates only to the level of words in this categorisation, while stress, rhythm, intonation and other suprasegmental features help to convey the tone. Segmentals may therefore have very limited importance in interactional terms. Smith and Nelson (1985), quoted above, claim that problems of miscommunication arise more often in terms of comprehensibility and interpretability, rather than intelligibility (word recognition). Suprasegmentals relate more to the former levels and may therefore again be assigned greater overall importance than segmentals.

A glance at books on pronunciation teaching and phonetics shows a topsy-turvy approach, in view of the above conclusions. Typically, consonant and vowel pronunciation is introduced first, with stress, rhythm and intonation trailing in behind almost as afterthoughts. Even the term *suprasegmentals* implies secondary status to segmentals. Bolinger has criticised this, as follows:

> If the child could paint the picture, [rhythm and intonation] would be the wave on which the other components ride up and down; but the linguist is older and stronger, and has his way – he calls them suprasegmentals, and makes the wave ride on top of the ship. (Bolinger, 1961, quoted in Gilbert 1984:1–2)

This point is also made by Haycraft (chapter 6), who emphasises the importance of sentence stress in early pronunciation work.

14   Do we know everything about how English pronunciation works?

In terms of consonants and vowels (which, however, we have just said ought to be given less attention), it is fair to say that we already know all we need to know about how such sounds are produced; any problems confronting materials writers and teachers are in terms of converting this information into effective classroom procedures.

On the other hand, in terms of suprasegmentals (which we have just concluded are of great importance), the picture often seems to be that we do not even know the systems underlying speakers' control of stress, rhythm, intonation, etc. If we do not know what native speakers do, it is of course impossible to know what to teach or how to teach it.

In the field of rhythm, the question is even more basic. It is not so much 'what is the system underlying English rhythm?' as 'what is rhythm?' Less controversial is the fact that native English speech contains several features which are a direct result of its stress-based nature. Vaughan-Rees (chapter 5) presents a number of enjoyable classroom exercises which focus on these aspects of simplification (such as elision, assimilation, weak forms and liaison).

In the field of intonation, ELT has generally followed the phonological descriptions of O'Connor and Arnold (1973), Halliday (1970) and Brazil *et al.* (1980). Descriptions of English intonation have tended to become simpler. O'Connor and Arnold's analysis contained 10 main categories; Halliday's used five; and Brazil *et al.*'s description is based on a major two-way distinction. Brazil *et al.*'s account is also more unified than previous analyses, in that different pitch patterns are accounted for purely in discoursal terms, whereas previous analyses involved mixtures of the levels of attitude, emphasis, grammar, and so on. Kenworthy (chapter 7) shows how exercises written primarily for other grammatical purposes may be exploited for the teaching of the interactive discoursal dimension of English intonation.

15   Are any important aspects of English pronunciation left out of pronunciation teaching?

Abercrombie (1967:89) divides the stream of speech into three strands. Firstly, there are the *segments*, namely the vowels and consonants of a language. As we have already seen, these have been well described by phoneticians and are generally covered adequately in pronunciation teaching.

Secondly, there are the *voice dynamic* features of loudness, pitch and length. These combine to give the suprasegmentals of stress, rhythm and intonation. We have already noted that there are differing theories regarding these suprasegmentals, and consequently their treatment in ELT classes is often lacking.

Thirdly, there is the *voice quality* strand. Voice quality is the more or less permanent auditory background that permeates the stream of a person's speech. It may characterise the person himself, his social status, various personality traits, his regional accent and, of importance in the present discussion, his native language. At present, it would be true to say that voice quality is totally absent from most ELT classes.

The argument for the adoption of voice quality in pronunciation classes is that languages differ in voice quality, and that it is a very pervasive aspect of pronunciation, underlying, as it does, all vocal output. If a learner can be trained to abandon the long-term settings of his or her native language and switch to those of the L2 (to 'get into gear', as Honikman (1964) called it), then this large-scale adjustment will facilitate small-scale changes needed in the articulation of the particular vowels and consonants of the language. Jenner (chapter 4) outlines exercises for introducing voice quality into pronunciation classes.

16   How can pronunciation teaching be integrated into ELT?

My point, in posing this question, is not so much to discuss whether pronunciation *ought* to be a part of each lesson plan as to point out that pronunciation necessarily *does* appear in each lesson. The same can be said of grammar, vocabulary, and all other levels of language. As soon as the teacher starts the lesson by saying 'Good morning', the students are exposed to utterances of English, which they will take as exemplars of good pronunciation, correct grammar and appropriate vocabulary choice. In certain cases, this may constitute the majority of their exposure to the language. It is therefore as important that the teacher should speak with a good pronunciation as that he or she should speak grammatically.

However, it is not necessary that *explicit* pronunciation teaching should appear in every ELT lesson. Often any attention to pronunciation takes the form of remedial action as and when it is required. What is more important is that when pronunciation teaching does appear, it is integrated into the language as a whole and not studied as a phenomenon divorced from the process of communication.

There is a saying in ELT circles: 'a drill is a device for boring'. It is unfortunate that many attempts by teachers at pronunciation teaching take the form of drilling, and therefore lack interest. One of the major movements within ELT in the 1980s was away from teaching language as a formal system towards using language as a means of communicating in realistic tasks. Some writers (for example, Pica, 1984) claim that it is this failure to teach pronunciation communicatively, in meaningful exchange and problem-posing tasks, which accounts for the failure of much pronunciation teaching to date.

Celce-Murcia (1987:10) gives the following guidelines for the communicative teaching of pronunciation:

1   Identify your students' problem areas (different groups of students may have different problems).
2   Find lexical/grammatical contexts with many natural occurrences of the problem sound(s).
3   Develop communicative tasks that incorporate the word.
4   Develop at least three or four exercises so that you can recycle the problem and keep practising the target sound(s) with new contexts.

Celce-Murcia's guidelines and sample exercises seem to apply more to segmental than suprasegmental pronunciation. Kenworthy (chapter 7) shows how pronunciation may be integrated into exercises whose primary function is the teaching of grammar.

17   What about drama, simulations and role plays?

The interactive aspect of pronunciation, and other aspects of English, can also be emphasised by the use of drama techniques. In general, this relates more to the pronunciation levels of stress, intonation and voice quality, as well as the closely related non-verbal levels of gestures, facial expressions and posture. Actors require preliminary exercises in order to prepare them to make the adjustment necessary to assume behavioural characteristics different from their own. Similar exercises may be used to get students in the right frame of mind and state of relaxation to make the required adjustments in their pronunciation habits. Such exercises are described by Wessels and Lawrence (chapter 3) for pronunciation in general, and are touched on by Jenner (chapter 4) for the teaching of voice quality.

18   Must all pronunciation teaching use the aural medium?

It is understandable that teachers assume that the only way to teach pronunciation and listening comprehension, the productive and perceptual components of the oral/aural medium, is also through this medium. However, there are a wide range of visual techniques available for those students who find it difficult grasping such intangible and ethereal things as sounds. This is often the case for those students who do not have an alphabetic native language writing system such as Chinese and Japanese. My own contribution (chapter 11) discusses the use of various sorts of head diagrams in physiological descriptions of pronunciation. Marks (chapter 10) lists other more abstract techniques, many of them using Cuisenaire rods.

19   How useful might computers be?

There is scarcely any walk of life which has not been affected by the introduction of computers over the last 20 years or so. Computers are also used in ELT, and it is appropriate that ways should be explored for using them in pronunciation teaching. Computer displays of aspects of the speech signal such as pitch and intensity have been used for some years in the remedial treatment of pathological speech defects (such as deafness, cleft palate and the effects of strokes). The same displays are now available at affordable prices for the personal computers which most ELT schools have. Molholt (chapter 12) describes one such program, and examines the wealth of information which has now been made available to the ELT teacher for use in pronunciation work.

20   How do we test pronunciation?

Heaton (1988:5) writes 'both testing and teaching are so closely interrelated that it is virtually impossible to work in either field without being constantly concerned with the other'. Many exercises seem equally usable as practice material during teaching or as tests; the difference is one of purpose rather than nature. However, although many writers have discussed exercises for pronunciation teaching, very few have proposed rigorous tests of pronunciation.

Suffice it to say, as an example of this neglect, that since the start of the journal *Language Testing* in 1984, only one article has appeared specifically on the topic of pronunciation testing (as opposed to oral fluency, or attitudes to oral as against written testing). The author of that article submits that 'the measurement of pronunciation accuracy is in the dark ages when compared to measurement of other areas of competence' (Major, 1987:155).

In the preparation of this collection, four writers were approached to contribute a chapter on testing, but for various reasons were unable to. Much to my regret, the collection does not deal with this important aspect of the subject, beyond a few comments by Haycraft, and the overall observation that most of the exercises contained in the chapters could be used as tests.

References

Abercrombie, D. (1956) *Problems and Principles: Studies in the Teaching of English as a Second Language* Longmans Green, London. Extract also in A. Brown (ed., 1991), pp. 87–95.

Abercrombie, D. (1967) *Elements of General Phonetics* Edinburgh University Press.

Bolinger, D.L. (1961) *Forms of English* Harvard University Press, Cambridge, Mass.

Brazil, D., Coulthard, M. and Johns, C. (1980) *Discourse Intonation and Language Teaching* Longman, London.

Brown, A. (1988) 'Functional load and the teaching of pronunciation' *TESOL Quarterly* 22:593–606. Also in A. Brown (ed., 1991), pp. 211–224.

Brown, A. (1989) 'Models, standards, targets/goals and norms in pronunciation teaching' *World Englishes* 8:193–200.

Brown, A. (1991) *Pronunciation Models* Singapore University Press.

Brown, A. (ed., 1991) *Teaching English Pronunciation: A Book of Readings* Routledge, London.

Celce-Murcia, M. (1987) 'Teaching pronunciation as communication' in J. Morley (ed.) *Current Perspectives on Pronunciation* TESOL, Washington, DC, pp. 1–12.

Ellis, G. and Sinclair, B. (1989) *Learning to Learn English* Cambridge University Press.

Gilbert, J.D. (1984) *Clear Speech: Pronunciation and Listening Comprehension in American English* Cambridge University Press.

Halliday, M.A.K. (1970) *A Course in Spoken English: Intonation* Oxford University Press.

Hanna, P.R., Hodges, R.E. and Hanna, J.S. (1971) *Spelling: Structure and Strategies* Houghton Mifflin, Boston.

Haycraft, B. (1971) *The Teaching of Pronunciation: A Classroom Guide* Longman, London.

Heaton, J.B. (1988) *Writing English Language Tests* (2nd edition) Longman, London.

Herdan, G. (1958) 'The relation between the functional burdening of phonemes and the frequency of occurrence' *Language & Speech* 1:13.

Hill, G. (1982) 'English in Brunei: second language or foreign language?' *World Language English* 1:240–242.

Honikman, B. (1964) 'Articulatory settings' in D. Abercrombie *et al.* (eds.) *In Honour of Daniel Jones* Longman, London, pp. 73–84. Also in A. Brown (ed., 1991), pp. 276–287.

James, C. (1980) *Contrastive Analysis* Longman, London.

Kenworthy, J. (1987) *Teaching English Pronunciation* Longman, London.

Knowles, G. (1987) *Patterns of Spoken English* Longman, London.

Ladefoged, P. (1982) *A Course in Phonetics* (2nd edition) Harcourt Brace Jovanovich, New York.

Leather, J. (1983) 'Second-language pronunciation learning and teaching' *Language Teaching and Linguistics: Abstracts* 16:198–219.

Macauley, R. (1988) 'RP R.I.P.' *Applied Linguistics* 9:115–124.

MacCarthy, P. (1978) *The Teaching of Pronunciation* Cambridge University Press.

Major, R.C. (1987) 'Measuring pronunciation accuracy using computerized techniques' *Language Testing* 4:155–169.

Mehrabian, A. and Ferris, S.R. (1967) 'Influence of attitudes from nonverbal communication in two channels' *Journal of Consulting Psychology* 31:248–252.

Moag, R. (1982) 'English as a foreign, second, native, and basal language: a new taxonomy of English-using societies' in J.B. Pride (ed.) *New Englishes* Newbury House, Rowley, Mass., pp. 11–50.

Morley, J., Robinett, B.W. and Stevick, E.W. (1975) 'Round robin on the teaching of pronunciation', *TESOL Quarterly* 9:81–88.

O'Connor, J.D. and Arnold, G.F. (1973) *Intonation of Colloquial English* (2nd edition) Longman, London.

Pennington, M.C. and Richards, J.C. (1986) 'Pronunciation revisited' *TESOL Quarterly* 20:207–225.

Pica, T. (1984) 'Pronunciation activities with an accent on communication' *English Teaching Forum* 22(3):2–6. Also in A. Brown (ed., 1991), pp. 332–342.

Roach, P. (1983) *English Phonetics and Phonology: A Practical Course* Cambridge University Press.

Rogerson, P. and Gilbert, J.B. (1990) *Speaking Clearly* Cambridge University Press.

von Schon, C.V. (1987) 'The question of pronunciation' *English Teaching Forum* 25(4):22–27.

Shaw, W.D. (1981) 'Asian student attitudes towards English' in L.E. Smith (ed. 1981) *English for Cross-Cultural Communication* Macmillan, London, pp. 108–122. Also in L.E. Smith (ed., 1983) *Readings in English as an International Language* Pergamon, Oxford, pp. 21–33.

Smith, L.E. and Nelson, C. (1985) 'International intelligibility of English: directions and resources' *World Englishes* 4:333–342.

Strevens, P. (1974) 'A rationale for teaching pronunciation: the rival virtues of innocence and sophistication' *ELT Journal* 28:182–189. Also in A. Brown (ed., 1991), pp. 96–103.

Swan, M. and Smith, B. (1987) *Learner English: A Teacher's Guide to Interference and Other Problems* Cambridge University Press.

Temperley, M.S. (1983) 'The articulatory target for final -s clusters' *TESOL Quarterly* 17:421–436.

Temperley, M.S. (1987) 'Linking and deletion in final consonant clusters' in J. Morley (ed.) *Current Perspectives on Pronunciation: Practices Anchored in Theory* TESOL, Washington, DC, pp. 63–82.

Tench, P. (1981) *Pronunciation Skills* Macmillan, London.

Upward, C. (1988) *English Spelling and Educational Progress* CLIE Working Papers no. 11, CLIE/BAAL/LAGB, Birmingham.

Wells, J.C. and Colson, G. (1971) *Practical Phonetics* Pitman, London.

Chapter 2
Teaching Phonology to Teachers: The Phonology Element in Initial Training Courses

Lindsay Ross
BEET Language Centre, Bournemouth

Introduction

Many teachers find it difficult to *teach* pronunciation. They may give perfectly clear pronunciation models themselves when presenting new language, deal ably with the correction of pronunciation in the classroom, indicate rising or falling intonation, mark stress on new lexical items and so on. However, they do not have any kind of systematic approach to teaching pronunciation as a language area.

This is due to two factors. Firstly, the mystification of the whole area of phonology, with its unfamiliar terminology (*voiced bilabial fricative, suprasegmental, elision of alveolar plosives, stress-timed languages,* and so on) which may have no apparent practical application, and no systematic treatment in most coursebooks. Secondly, the way in which phonology is presented in teachers' initial training.

Phonology is often presented in Royal Society of Arts (RSA) (Preparatory) Certificate courses or Trinity College Certificate courses in three or four fairly indigestible lumps, on 'Vowels' or 'Stress and Intonation' for example, which may or may not be integrated with the rest of the course input, and with the teaching practice (TP).

A trainee who is (only just) coping with new ideas on classroom management, lesson planning, presentation and practice techniques, skills, lexis and textbooks, may well decide to prioritise what he or she sees as more immediately relevant to daily classroom survival, at the expense of consistent and systematic pronunciation work. The problem arises when phonology work is *not* tackled by a trainee at this level. If she does not practise teaching phonology in observed TP, when she can rely on the advice and help of experienced tutors, then she is highly unlikely to teach phonology after the training course, when she is working on her own in a school, perhaps without much help or support from the rest of the busy staff.

Thus the situation comes about where teachers, even at the level of

RSA Diploma, are inexperienced and nervous about the whole subject of phonology, and will try to avoid it at all costs.

This chapter lays out a model for introducing 'phon. and pron.' little by little during initial training. The model uses techniques which familiarise trainees with different aspects of phonology through discovery learning wherever possible. This approach makes concepts such as elision, assimilation or voiced/voiceless consonants less threatening. Experiencing the activities enables trainees to use them right away with EFL students in their TP. By spending five to 10 minutes every day on a phonology activity, the learning is seen as fun, while the new information is constantly recycled. At the same time, these short activities can act as 'warmers', or breaks in longer sessions, or can round off a topic without taking too much precious time away from other timetabled sessions. Four long sessions back up the short activities by covering the theory as well as any other techniques. In this way, trainees are introduced to the whole area gradually and painlessly. After each activity, trainees are asked to assess whether the activity could be used with EFL students, what the aim of it is, how to use it, possible problems such as instructions or resistance to new ideas, and the level at which the activity would be most appropriate.

I have found it useful to start with activities on connected speech or stress and intonation, then go on to sounds and combinations of sounds and finally return to the areas of stress and intonation. By this time a useful knowledge of transcription symbols has also been gained. In this way, trainees can see that the four areas are not unconnected. In addition, they have been able to use the first activities throughout the intervening TP.

Trainees are asked to keep a separate section of their folder or notebook in which to note these activities and any others they may observe or try out during the course. This provides them with a bank of techniques to refer to and expand on in their future teaching.

Many of these mini-activities have been adapted from different original sources over the years – I take no credit for having 'invented' all of them. I have laid them out here as a number of consecutive activities and input sessions, which can be used either on a four-week course, or throughout a longer evening course.

Activity 1

Connected speech game
Trainees are given pairs of cards to discuss. These include phrases like *short list/shortbread/shortcake* or *10 o'clock/10 pence/10 gallon hat* or *good afternoon/good morning/good grief!*, and cover several ways in which sounds are affected by those next to them. This activity forms part of a session on raising language awareness. It is designed to introduce the idea of phonology through a non-threatening, discovery-

based activity, and at the same time to begin discussion of the whole idea of spoken *vs.* written English. At this point, no terminology is introduced, but reference is made to the activity in one of the later Applied Phonology sessions.

Activity 2

Matching stress game
Make a set of eight pairs of cards, a different one for each trainee (assuming that there are 16 on the course).
e.g.

o O	rapport
O o	concept
O o o	lexical
o O o	linguistic
o O o o	activity
o o O o	introduction
o o o O o	pronunciation
o O o o o	communicative

Trainees are given a card each. The card either has a stress pattern (e.g. O o o, o O) or a word with corresponding stress (*lexical, rapport*). Trainees have to walk around the room grunting the sounds (MMM-mm-mm, da-DA) represented by the stress pattern or word (it is important that trainees *grunt* the pattern of the word rather than *say* the word itself) until they find their partner, who should be grunting the same pattern. The short discussion afterwards focuses on how this can be applied to new vocabulary or to introducing students to the idea of stress in words.

A useful follow-up homework task is to give out a list of 'EFL teaching words', such as *elicit, presentation, phonology, nominate, interaction, exponent*. Trainees have to (*a*) state how many syllables the word has; (*b*) mark the main stress or match it to one of the patterns in the game; and (*c*) check they understand the EFL meaning of the word.

Activity 3

Marking stress on given words
On an OHP transparency are two columns of words, totalling the number of trainees in the group. The trainees are put into two teams, and have to mark the stressed syllable (on the projected image) as quickly as possible. The first team to finish wins. This extends the work done on the previous day, and can be referred to in the session on board organisation, as well as giving trainees practice in identifying and

marking stress in words for TP. Any list of words is appropriate. For example, if there is a TP session on reading and listening comprehension in the near future, then words from the text can be used, or key words connected with one of the day's input sessions.

Activity 4

The tutor puts two stress patterns on the board, for example

o o O   o O o

In pairs, trainees supply further examples of phrases or sentences, or pairs of phrases or sentences, which fit the different patterns, for example,

o o O	o O o
can you TYPE?	can YOU type?
what is THAT?	what IS that?
I like SQUID	I HATE it

If trainees find this very difficult, the tutor can feed in prompts, such as *name, too*, or extend the number of patterns. This is designed to show how shifts in stress affect meaning and to introduce intonation patterns.

Activity 5

/uː/, /iː/, /ʊ/, /ɪ/, (plus /ʃ/, /s/, /p/, /d/). This forms an introduction of the first phonetic symbols, based on Adrian Underhill's 'Sound Foundations', using a chart of phonetic symbols (or not). A video of this technique is available from ITTI, London. The tutor mouths these sounds silently, *without making the sounds*, and students supply the sound itself. This encourages students to think about the shape of their lips and position of tongue and teeth (shown with hands) rather than attempt to recreate, through the interference of their own L1, an aurally perceived sound. I start with these sounds because /uː/ and /iː/ are very easy to distinguish, especially at this early stage, when students might still be a little surprised at what the tutor expects them to do. Once students are producing the sounds, then different combinations of sounds can be pointed out, e.g. *soup, deep, should*. The tutor can use her hands to indicate the length of vowels, as well as whether she wants students' voices to go up or down.

At the end of this short session, it is a good idea to discuss what has been done and the fact that the **students** were discovering the sounds required and developing muscular trace memory, as well as how and when this technique could be introduced in the classroom.

Activity 6

The tutor starts by revising the sounds introduced the previous day, and introduces the following: /ɔː/, /ɒ/, /ɔɪ/, /ɑː/, /æ/, aɪ/, (plus /t/, /m/, /n/). In addition, she can point to one symbol and mouth several sounds. Students say 'yes' or 'no' according to whether the sound she mouths is the sound she is pointing to.

Activity 7

The tutor continues with sound work, recycling those sounds already taught and introducing /ʌ/, /e/, /ɜː/, /ə/, /eɪ/. By now, trainees can easily come out in front of the class and lead this activity, with the pointing and the 'yes/no' answers, just as students in the EFL classroom can.

Activity 8 (Applied Phonology 1)

/əʊ/, /aʊ/, /ɪə/, /eə/, /ʊə/. At this point, it is usually time for a session on Applied Phonology, to start drawing some ideas together. After a short discussion on the way the symbols have been introduced, we look at the efficacy of this approach and how the trainees now feel about phonology (hopefully not so nervous!). We also discuss why teachers of English need to know about phonology, the extent to which students of EFL may or may not need to know about it, and look briefly at some of the more common spelling/sound correspondences. As trainees have become quite familiar with transcription by now, I use an OHP transparency with several *-ough* words (*rough, cough, hiccough, though, through, lough, bough*) written on it. The transcription beside each word is covered, and trainees supply the transcription, and check their answers later. We also look at words like *bear/dear, loose/goose/ choose/lose, rose/dose, dead/bead, meat/feet* etc., and decide which sounds are different in each.

I go on to invite them to categorise vowels in any way they want to. This leads to making distinctions between long and short vowel sounds, and monophthongs/diphthongs/triphthongs. At this point we also discuss phonological transcription(s), where phonemics fits in, the different length of /æ/ in *back* and *bag*, and possibly even accentual problems for teachers. Trainees then define how vowels are made and what distinguishes one from another (for example, shape of lips, position of tongue). At this point I may refer to the trapezium chart with vowel sounds plotted on it which is common in many books on phonology, although personally I find it extremely unclear. After deciding which particular pairs of vowel sounds may cause problems for EFL students, we look at some practical techniques based on mininal pairs which will help students to (*a*) distinguish between different vowel sounds and (*b*) produce those sounds. Activities include the following:

1   The teacher focuses on two sounds, for example /ɪ/ and /iː/, and establishes a different signal for each (e.g. raise your right hand if you hear /iː/, don't raise either hand if you hear /ɪ/). The teacher then – quite quickly – says a series of words, such as *sit, hit, heat, hit, seat, sit, pit, peat, peat, peal, pill, hill, hill, heal*, checking after each one to see if students have made the correct response or not. (It works quite well if the tutor actually makes the required response, after a second's delay. This way students can also see whether they were right or not.)

With a lively group, then the instructions for this game can be stand up/sit down instead of raise one hand. If you have a quieter, more serious group, they might respond more readily to, for example, raising a yellow card for /ɪ/ and a blue card for /iː/.

2   The teacher focuses on two or three sounds, e.g. the /æ/, /ʌ/, /ɑː/ vowels in *cap, cup, carp*. She then reads out a list of numbered words. Students have to put the *number* of the word (not the word itself) under the appropriate symbol. (If the students are not familiar with symbols, this is an easy way to practise one or two at a time. Alternatively, the teacher can do this activity by using words which have the sounds at the top of each column.) For example, the teacher reads: 1. *hat* 2. *heart* 3. *hut* 4. *cat* 5. *cart* 6. *cut* 7. *part* 8. *putt* 9. *pat* 10. *ban*. Students fill in:

/æ/	/ʌ/	/ɑː/
1	3	2
4	6	5
9	8	7
10		

These activities can clearly be used with any vowel or consonant sounds the teacher might feel are necessary for her group.

3   The teacher prepares a sheet with simple drawings of objects, such as *bird/beard, pen/pan/pin, hut/hat, bike/beak*. The teacher names one of the groups and the students circle it. Students can then compare their results in pairs, and produce similar drawings (or use the same ones again) to work on together, one saying the word, the other circling.

Activity 9

Rhyme exercise from song
Trainees are asked to supply words that rhyme with particular given words, e.g. *law, lie, lay*, or are given a list of words which they have to match to the correct sound (e.g. *dawn, for, four, arm, my, soar, rye, awe, scorn, bay, born, yawn, neigh, fey*) and go on to examine spelling/sound relationship. This is done in a session on integrated skills and is one of several exploitation exercises leading up to a song which uses these

rhymes. In this way, we can discuss different ways of exploiting songs linguistically (rather than just listening, or listening and filling in gaps) while showing how phonology work can be integrated into any lesson, and can also be used to provide exposure to new lexis before another related task.

Activity 10 (Applied Phonology 2)

/tʃ/, /dʒ/, /f/, /v/, /ð/, /θ/. These sounds are practised in the same way as before, and different combinations of sounds are pointed out. This second input session on Applied Phonology starts with trainees classifying consonants into two main categories: they usually come up with voiced and voiceless. Trainees are then invited to complete a chart which shows consonant sounds plus their place and manner of articulation. Some of the spaces are blank, but not so many as to make the charts overpowering. This is a quick and simple way to introduce some of the terminology and create a reference table, e.g.

VOICED	VOICELESS	PLACE	MANNER
b	p	bilabial	plosive
g	k	velar	
d		alveolar	
	θ		fricative
	f		fricative
z		alveolar	
m			nasal
		velar	nasal

If trainees find this too difficult, I do not spend too long on it but put up a completed OHP transparency which they can use to fill in their own chart. Alternatively, the chart can be organised as an information gap exercise, to be completed in pairs. We then go on to discuss common student problems with consonants and look at some activities to help them.

First we examine physical aids, such as:

  (i) touching windpipes to feel the difference between voiced and voiceless consonants;
 (ii) touching fingers to lips while saying *this, then, there, thick, thin* and checking to see if the finger is wet or not;
(iii) holding a piece of paper up and comparing what happens when you say /b/ and /p/ as in *bin* (unaspirated) and *pin* (aspirated) (this can be done with a lit match – if your students are of an appropriate age!);
 (iv) using mirrors to see how they move their lips and tongue can also be very effective, particularly for /b/ *vs.* /v/, or /r/ *vs.* /l/ – but the tutor will have to ensure that the trainees (or students) actually *do* look in the mirror at their mouths, and not at the teacher.

Secondly, we look at minimal pair exercises, and trainees are asked to complete lists of minimal pairs for /s/ *vs.* /z/, /p/ *vs.* /b/, /b/ *vs.* /v/, or /d/, /ð/, /t/ etc., and to identify which language groups might have trouble with which sounds.

Another useful technique, for production this time, is one developed by a colleague, Jill Manwaring, whereby students refer to a list of minimal pairs, and, working together, take it in turns to mouth silently one of the words, which the other has to identify, e.g.

	A	B
1	sick	thick
2	some	thumb
3	path	pass
4	that	sat
	or	
1	fine	wine
2	will	fill
3	when	fen
4	fir	were

Clearly, there will be some exaggeration when mouthing the words, but this serves to heighten awareness of where and how the sounds are formed. The 'lip-reader' should identify the word by saying *1a, 4b, 3a* etc., so that if there is any disagreement, the students can work out whether the word has been mispronounced or misunderstood. Charts can be devised to tackle the particular problems of the students in a group, and different charts can be used simultaneously or one at a time.

Finally we look at consonant clusters, and which ones might cause particular problems, such as /str-/, /-θs/ or /-sps/ as in *stream, paths* and *grasps*.

Activity 11

Watusi Rodeo
This is a song by The Waterboys and is part of a session on songs, showing how exploitation of a song might be phonological. Trainees make a list of animals, then listen to the song and check which ones are on their lists, and match the names of these animals to (*a*) stress patterns and (*b*) the sound of their plural endings. This activity also fits in with the input sessions on teaching lexis, in which we look at stress in words, and trainees are invited to contribute any phonological 'rules' they may be aware of, such as stress (*a*) in words of foreign origin, with endings such as *-oo, -oon, -ette*, etc. or (*b*) before particular endings such as *-ity, -sophy, -logy, -tion, -ian* and so on. These can be usefully provided on a handout for trainees to work out their own rules, or can provide the basis for a 'Match similar patterns' exercise. Trainees can also decide what happens to words which start with prefixes, and words

which have different stress patterns as verbs *vs.* nouns/adjectives, e.g. *contrast, export, suspect.*

Activity 12 (Applied Phonology 3)

Really?
Trainees think of three ways of saying the word *really* and in pairs discuss different meanings/functions of intonation patterns. This can also be done with other short words such as *where, yes* and *no*, and can be used to highlight the relationship between the length of vowel sounds and change in voice pitch.

In the session on stress and intonation, I start by giving out the script of a taped text (any short clear text will do), and ask trainees, first individually then in pairs, to mark which words are most important in terms of meaning. Then we listen to the text and compare what is said with the anticipated stress marked. They then listen again and decide whether pitch goes up or down on each marked stress, compare their answers with each other, and then with the taped text. At this point we discuss different theories of intonation, but in particular, we look at what is shared information and what is new. I have found Jenner's (1988) article to be very useful back-up reading for this session. Trainees might also complete the following worksheet which can serve as a reference:

COMPLETE THE FOLLOWING STATEMENTS WITH *up, down* or *down/up, up/down*:

    1   Intonation in yes/no questions usually goes ___
    2   Intonation in business-like '*wh*' questions usually goes ___
    3   Intonation in incomplete or two-part sentences usually goes ___
    4   Intonation in contrast sentences usually goes ___
    5   Intonation in statements expressing reservation usually goes ___

LOOK AT THE FOLLOWING DIALOGUE:

    Q: What did the boss say when you saw him?
    A: I didn't see him.

NOW MARK THE STRESS IN THE FOLLOWING VERSIONS OF THE REPLY:

    I didn't see him (Jim did)
    I didn't see him (I spoke to him on the phone)
    I didn't see him (He wasn't there)
    I didn't see him (I saw his assistant)

This worksheet can be used for discussion of the relationship between intonation and meaning. Other activities include the following:

1   Trainees are given a short piece of text and mark the intonation according to a tape of the text.

2   Two-part sentences: Trainees write three short statements and read them to their partner, who decides whether the sentence is complete or not according to the intonation.

3   In pairs, trainees role play one visiting the other, going into their house, sitting down, and then starting to argue. However, all this is done without words, using numbers only.

4   Trainees read a short dialogue together, which is transcribed without any punctuation (the works of Harold Pinter can be very useful for this) and see how intonation and stress add to the meaning of the words.

Activity 13

Trainees underline all three-syllable words in a text and then compare their stress patterns.

Activity 14 (Applied Phonology 4)

In this session I refer trainees to the exercise from the beginning of the course, and we discuss elision, assimilation, catenation and the weak and strong forms of words. I give them a handout containing some isolated words (such as *had, of, and, some*), and some in phrases (*he had a bad fall, a bag of chips, fish and chips, I saw some strange things*) and ask them to transcribe the highlighted word in both cases. We then look at what happens to words such as *library, secretary, family, potato,* and *canary* (the /ə/ vowel is very weak, and may disappear altogether, so that *library* has only two syllables). Other activities include the following:

1   *Revision of symbols*
Half the class underlines the weak sounds while the other half underlines aspects of linked speech in a given short text, which can be written or spoken. The class then pairs up and the two trainees in each pair compare their different work.

2   *Linking*
Trainees draw linking arrows underneath words on a transcribed text, wherever the end of one word is linked to the beginning of the next, e.g. *He went up those steps.*

Activity 15

Trainees think of as many different sounds as possible for different digraphs, for example *ea* (*meat, great, threat,* etc.), *ou, x,* or, conversely, as many different spellings as possible for the same sound, e.g. /eə/, /ʃ/

(*ship, charade, sugar, mission*).

Phonology is also discussed in other input sessions, for example, stress in sentences when talking about conducting choral repetition, or stress and intonation in new language items in language analysis sessions.

Another approach which has had a positive effect is the introduction of phonology self-access work, which trainees, teachers, and teachers on refresher courses can work at according to their own interest and time available. This self-access 'box' consists of short questions (such as those in Brita Haycraft's regular column in the journal *Practical English Teaching*) or recognition/transcription exercises, with accompanying taped material, with answers on the back of each activity sheet.

Conclusion

Clearly there is room for improvement in this model, but reactions have been favourable and trainees have started using techniques immediately in their teaching practice, and have paid more attention to pronunciation in general. In feedback, many have commented on their feelings – surprise at enjoying phonology work, not feeling threatened and appreciating the number of practical techniques they experience and then teach. I have been pleased to see this approach being adopted in other teacher training centres, where it seems to have had good results, so that more and more EFL teachers are completing their initial training with a positive attitude to teaching pronunciation and an interest in phonology in general.

Reference

Jenner, B. (1988) 'Teaching intonation without specialised materials' *Speak Out!* (Newsletter of the IATEFL Phonology Special Interest Group) 3:17–20.

Chapter 3

Using Drama Voice Techniques in the Teaching of Pronunciation

Charlyn Wessels *Stevenson College, Edinburgh*
Kate Lawrence *University of Edinburgh*

Introduction

The voice and speech routines used in the theatre by actors to prepare for a variety of roles can offer us as language teachers many useful techniques to incorporate in the teaching of pronunciation. Drama voice techniques go far beyond traditional ways of teaching pronunciation, such as listening to model speakers on a cassette and repeating what is heard. They include concentrating on the shape of the mouth, posture, the mechanics of breathing, facial expressions and body language. They emphasise warming up the organs of speech through tongue exercises and increasing pitch range through intonation exercises. They also create awareness in learners that speech is a whole series of inter-related events, and that the vocal flexibility needed to attain good pronunciation in a target language is the result of experience, lots of practice, and attention to many small but important factors.

In classes where these techniques are incorporated, they help to reduce the stress that is often a feature of speech production in a foreign language. The demands made of students in the language class are often similar to the demands of public speaking in front of a critical audience, and so it is important to find ways of reducing this type of stress. Drama voice techniques are fun, they help to relax the learners, and they build empathy as well – all of which help to reduce stress. These techniques also increase overall learner confidence, because they help learners to speak clearer, louder and in a variety of tones and registers, all of which are tied to appropriate posture and body language. Lastly, they offer learners valuable and practical insights into the mechanics of speech by stimulating awareness of the organs of articulation and the amount of control the learners have over them.

Types of drama voice techniques

In the appendix to Clifford Turner's (1977) book, *Voice and Speech in the Theatre*, Malcolm Morrison outlines typical voice and speech routines for the actor. These include the following:

1   *Relaxation and posture*
Exercises designed to release tension. When we are tense, our stiff bodies and hunched shoulders impair our breathing, and without breath control we cannot use our voices fully.

2   *Breathing*
Learning to control and utilise breathing fully. 'The breath is seen to be the foundation upon which utterance is built,' says Turner (1977).

3   *Tone*
Learning to use the resonators of the voice, that is, the way in which air vibrates in the hollows of the pharynx, mouth and nose, to create particular tones, for example, bright or dull, rich or thin, hard or soft. It is a speaker's tone that helps us to identify her or him over the telephone, even before s/he has told us her/his name.

4   *Pitch*
Exercises which practise the rise and fall of the voice. In language teaching, the rising and falling pattern of pitch is called intonation. Actors learn to hum, chant or sing in rising or falling pitch, as shown in this example:

```
                                                  high
                                          really
                                     go
                               voice
                    my
               make
          can
  I
          can
               make
                    my
                         voice
                              fall
                                    really
                                        low
```

Drama voice techniques offer a range of activities designed to sensitise the learner to the value and function of intonation.

5 *Articulation*

Reciting tongue-twisters, chants, or bits of poetry to secure clear speech. These exercises are also called 'vocal warm-ups', because they help to exercise the muscles of the mouth and tongue, thereby leading to greater articulatory agility. They can also help learners to distinguish between related sounds, by letting them chant tongue-twisters like 'She sells sea-shells on the sea-shore', or snatches of poetry which include sounds that are difficult for speakers of a particular language.

Apart from these voice and speech routines, there is also a range of drama activities which are aimed specifically at building confidence and improving projection, that is, the loudness and clarity of the voice. We also use choral poetry and singing in our classes, as well as 'rapping', which we first used in a drama option class at Stevenson College in Edinburgh to teach rhythm to learners of English. The chapter ends with an example of a rap and the insights we have gained from using them in our classes.

Sample activities

Most of these sample activities can be used at all levels. They can be used as warm-up exercises at the beginning of any lesson, or as part of specific pronunciation lessons. In all of them, the teacher is an active participant and serves as the main model for the class.

1 *Relaxation and posture*

These exercises can either be done seated or standing. Correct posture means either sitting or standing up straight, shoulders relaxed and not hunched, and head upright, focusing on something at eye-level. Any basic stretching exercises work well, but it helps the class if the physical exercises are contextualised. For example:

(i) looking at something on the ceiling, on the floor, or watching a tennis match (to relax the neck and head);
(ii) reaching for something on a high shelf, conducting an orchestra (arms and shoulders);
(iii) giving a loud yawn, stretching while doing so (arms, shoulders, chest and face);
(iv) making the face as big as possible, and then scrunching it up as small as possible (to relax the face muscles);
(v) smiling broadly, then wiping the smile away and throwing it at someone else in the class, who 'catches' it by smiling broadly in turn before wiping it away and throwing it at someone else (to relax the mouth and cheeks).

The teacher does these exercises together with the class, while talking the learners through the exercises. It is important to explain that these exercises, by relaxing and warming up the organs of articulation, prepare the learners for the breathing and voice exercises that are to follow.

2   *Breathing and resonance*

When doing breathing exercises, it is important to stress the need for correct lateral breathing, that means, the ribs should move outwards from the diaphragm, without raising the shoulders. It helps to visualise the lungs filling up with air from the bottom, rather like filling a glass with water from a tap. A basic breathing exercise is breathing in for a count of three, holding the air inside for three, and releasing the air for three. When this basic breathing exercise has been done four times, go into the following resonance exercises:

(i)   inhale, and let out the air on a long *aaaah* /ɑː/;
(ii)   inhale, and let out the air on a long *ooooh* /uː/;
(iii)   inhale, and let out the air on a long *eeeee* /iː/;
(iv)   combine the above with *mmmm* and *nnnn*, e.g. *mmmmaaaa, mmmmooo, mmmmeee*;
(v)   practise the above combinations by starting very softly, making it louder, and then becoming soft again; they can also be practised with falling and rising pitch, e.g. starting high and making the voice fall as low as possible;
(vi)   to finish, sing an easy tune which contains some pitch variation, e.g. *London's Burning*.

Once the learners have done these breathing and resonance exercises, the teacher can demonstrate the amount of control a learner can exercise over longer utterances through breath control by using a sentence extension activity. Here is an example of an 'elastic' sentence, a sentence that grows progressively longer, but uses the same amount of air each time:

(i)   inhale, and say *We went to the theatre last night.*
(ii)   inhale, and say *We went to the theatre last night to see my sister.*
(iii)   inhale, and say *We went to the theatre last night to see my sister in the role of Ophelia.*
(iv)   inhale, and say *We went to the theatre last night to see my sister in the role of Ophelia in 'Hamlet' by William Shakespeare.*

3   *Stress and intonation awareness activities*

(a)   *Counting and emotions*
The learners start by counting up to 12. Then they repeat the count, but they are instructed to say each third number with surprise, or impatience, or great pleasure, or anger. Each time, they count up to 12, so that for example the numbers three, six, nine and 12 are expressed with surprise. They are asked to imagine a context for each emotion

expressed, e.g. 'your mother has just walked into the room' for surprise. Learners find it easier to express these emotions if they face a partner, using the correct facial expressions and gestures where needed.

(b) *'Give me the letter.' 'No.'*
The learners are put into pairs, and asked to practise this simple dialogue in many different ways, e.g. aggressively, pleadingly, flirtatiously, coldly and politely. Much of the time, it is the way in which *'No'* is said that will dictate how *'Give me the letter'* will be said. Other dialogues which can be treated in the same way are the following:

> 'I love you.' 'Oh really?'
> 'That's enough.' 'OK.'

(c) *Gibberish or one-word only conversations*
Also done in pairs. Each learner picks a nonsense word or sound, e.g. *brum-brum, zenzo-zenzo,* or a single word like *shoe, toffee,* or *bed.* They have a conversation with their partners using only that word or sound. Once they have got used to the idea, they can be given specific situations to talk about, e.g. complaining about a nasty person or planning a surprise party.

(d) *Why won't you take me to the disco tonight?*
First, the teacher writes the sentence on the board. Then s/he shifts the stress as follows:

> WHY won't you take me to the disco tonight?
> Why won't YOU take me to the disco tonight?
> Why won't you take ME to the disco tonight?
> Why won't you take me to the DISCO tonight?
> Why won't you take me to the disco TONIGHT?

Then individual students take turns to ask the teacher these questions, shifting the stress each time as indicated. The teacher gives appropriate answers to indicate the change in meaning each time, e.g.

> I can't afford it.
> Jack's taking you to the disco tonight.
> I'm taking Sue to the disco tonight.
> I'd prefer to go to the theatre.
> There's a private function at the disco tonight.

Finally, the students pair off and practise the dialogues themselves.

(e) *Hummingbirds*
Use any short piece of English text. Read out the text to the class one sentence at a time, or play it if a tape is available. With lips closed, the class has to 'hum' the intonation pattern of the text, imitating the model as closely as possible. This simple procedure can be followed whenever a student is having difficulty with the tone of the utterance. By

'humming' and not having to worry about the words, s/he can concentrate on the tone pattern.

4   *Articulation exercises*

We have used articulation exercises successfully in our classes, particularly as preparation for rhythm exercises. Each 'vocal warm-up' is repeated three to five times, with increasing speed and volume. Students will find it easier to do these exercises if they do some 'face-loosening' exercises first. In addition to the ones already described above, we also use an exercise devised by Beatrice Honikman (1964), who used it to help her class of French students achieve the correct articulatory setting for English. The students are instructed as follows:

> Stick out your tongue and make it pointed. Now try to make it concave. Draw your tongue back into your mouth until the pointed tip rests behind the upper teeth. Close your mouth, but not tightly. Relax your lips. Relax your face. Swallow, and say the sounds /t,d,n,l/.

Once the learners are 'in gear' for English, they do the articulation exercises. We have found that they genuinely sound more English after the above exercise.

Here are five samples, and the language groups for whom they are particularly useful:

(a) *Look at the windmills whirling in the wind.* /w/ (German, Urdu, Scandinavian, Turkish)
(b) *The tip of the tongue, the teeth and the lips.* /t,ð,θ/ (all)
(c) *Bet you're very worried about your brother Wilfred.* /b,v,w/ (Spanish)
(d) *Armless Hannah hurried home after harmless Allie.* /h/ (French and Italian)
(e) *Red leather, yellow leather.* /r,l/ (Japanese and Chinese)

5   *Building confidence and improving projection*

(a) *Split dialogues*

The learners are asked to pair off, and to devise a two-line dialogue, for example:

> A: I'm afraid you're sitting in my seat.
> B: Oh sorry, I thought it was free.

All those with initiations are put on one side of the room, and the others with the responses on the other side. They stand with their backs to one another. The initiators have to say their parts loudly and clearly, so that their partners can respond correctly. They are asked not to shout, but simply to speak clearly and to take a deep breath before they start. Easy poems can also be split up and treated in this way. Each student has a different (numbered) line of the poem, and has to say it at the appropriate moment to maintain the rhythm of the poem.

(b) *Simultaneous conversations*
In pairs, the learners talk simultaneously on a topic previously decided, e.g. what they are planning to do that night. They have to make eye-contact throughout, but essentially they need to concentrate on their own voices. Alternatively, only one person does the talking, but his/her partner should look at him/her in a particular way, e.g. critically, angrily, lovingly, smiling broadly. It is a real test of confidence to keep talking while being stared at in an intimidating manner!

(c) *Laughing, crying and singing a dialogue*
The learners can either read a selected dialogue, or have an ordinary conversation on a topic of their choice. Then they are asked to repeat the dialogue as if it is extremely funny. They should laugh their way through the dialogue. Next, they are asked to do it as though they are very sad, and they should sob and cry their way through the dialogue. Finally, they can sing the dialogue in a style of their choice – pop, folk, opera, country and western and so on. Another variant of this exercise is to have the conversation as quickly or as slowly as possible.

6 *Rhythm through rapping*

To 'rap' simply means to talk or chat with someone. Authentic rap is spontaneous, strongly rhythmic and rhyming speech which is performed – usually by one person – to a basic 4/4 beat accompaniment. It seems to have been a feature of many black American immigrant communities but really took off in the 1970s when it surfaced in New York among young people. Spoken and part-sung raps are a form of street and disco art.

The raps we have written to use in our teaching are written in colloquial British English with some common American contractions, e.g. 'gonna' and 'gotta'. They retain most of the features of authentic raps – they use rhyme, repetition and simple structures, and they all work to a basic 4/4 beat. Most of them are written to be performed as dialogues, for more interaction and fun. Here is one example:

WAITING

Boys: *I've kept you waiting, I'm sorry, I'm sorry*
   I've kept you waiting, I'm sorry, I'm sorry

Girls: *What's your story this time? I've been here since nine!*
   What's your story this time? I've been here since nine!

   Well the car broke down, now you're wearing a frown
   Oh baby, please say you'll forgive me today
   I've kept you waiting, I'm sorry, I'm sorry
   I've kept you waiting, I'm sorry, I'm sorry.

   When I make a date, you're always late
   I sit here and wait while you procrastinate

> *Your excuses are thin; you must think I'm dim*
> *It's the car, or your watch, or you've cracked your shin!*
>
> *I've kept you waiting, I'm sorry, I'm sorry*
> *I've kept you waiting, I'm sorry, I'm sorry*
>
> *Oh, shut up and buy me a drink!*

Raps are meant to be performed – that is, said out loud, with accompanying gestures and facial expressions. So students need to prepare and practise them to make sure they produce a clear, correctly stressed performance. And raps are fun: speaking to a beat makes the experience much more dynamic and 'less like work', which is why they appeal to younger students who are familiar with them from the pop and disco scene. Some students do not like singing because they can't keep to a tune, but everybody can speak.

The basic 4/4 beat accompanying raps can be set up in a variety of ways:

(a)   standing, students stamp out the beat with their feet, moving from one foot to the other:

STAMP   STAMP

1   2   3   4

(b)   seated, students tap out the beat with their feet – twice on the one foot, and once (but holding it for a count of two) with the other:

tap–tap STAMP

1 2   3   4

(c)   seated, students slap their thighs twice and clap their hands (again, holding the clap for a count of two):

slap–slap CLAP

1   2   3 4

(d)   seated at their desks, students tap their desks twice and then clap their hands:

tap–tap CLAP

1 2   3   4

(e)   if the students find clapping and rapping simultaneously very difficult, then the rhythm accompaniment found on portable electronic keyboards can also be used.

For example, once the beat has been set up by the class, the first line of *Waiting* could be accompanied as follows:

Class   slap–slap CLAP (4 times to set up the beat), then:

I've kept you waiting, I'm sorry, I'm sorry
slap–slap CLAP   slap–slap CLAP

Or, if it is performed with the students standing, the accompanying beat could be as follows:

I've kept you waiting, I'm sorry, I'm sorry

STAMP STAMP   STAMP STAMP

Note that some students will find it difficult to concentrate on maintaining the beat and saying the words at the same time. Such students should be told to say the words, while the teacher and the rest of the class maintain the beat.

We use raps mainly to teach pronunciation, particularly stress and features of rhythm like weak forms and link-up. But they can also be used to teach specific grammar points, e.g. the simple present and present perfect as in the example above. Raps also practise vocabulary in appropriate contexts. And because they involve natural and unforced repetition, they provide painless and memorable natural 'drills'.

In a special pronunciation class, a selection of these drama voice techniques can be used to prepare the class for the main focus of the lesson, which might be working on specific problem sounds or practising intonation. But they can also be used as part of any language lesson that involves speech, either as warm-up activities or to promote vocal confidence.

References

Hayes, Suzanne (1984) *Drama as a Second Language* National Extension College, Cambridge.

Honikman, Beatrice (1964) 'Articulatory Settings' in *In Honour of Daniel Jones* (eds. Abercrombie *et al.*) Longmans Green, London.

Smith, Stephen (1984) *The Theatre Arts and the Teaching of Second Languages* Addison Wesley, London.

Turner, J. Clifford (1977) *Voice and Speech in the Theatre* (revised by M. Morrison) Black, London.

Wessels, Charlyn (1987) *Drama* Oxford Resource Series, Oxford University Press.

Wessels, Charlyn and Lawrence, Kate *Pronunciation* Unpublished manuscript.

Chapter 4
The English Voice

Bryan Jenner
Christ Church College, Canterbury

Introduction

The teaching of pronunciation has traditionally concerned itself with details. Most pronunciation manuals and teaching books contain exhaustive descriptions of all the separate sound segments of a language and how they differ from each other. They also provide exercises designed to ensure that the learner can produce pronunciations of *pin* and *bin*, or *ship* and *sheep*, which actually contrast with each other. This has led to a situation where many learners are quite capable of producing a full set of contrasting sound segments, or 'phonemes' (44 in the case of Standard British English), which are, on the one hand, clearly differentiated from each other, but which, on the other hand, sound entirely 'foreign' or 'un-English'. This chapter has two broad aims:

1   To identify those *general* features of pronunciation which underlie all the separate sounds of a language, and which enable us to recognise speakers as 'native' or 'non-native', irrespective of the clarity of their pronunciation; and
2   To suggest ways in which a more authentically English 'voice quality' (Laver, 1980), or 'setting' (Honikman, 1964), or 'articulatory basis' (Arnold and Hansen, 1979), might be developed.

There are a number of problems associated with the description and teaching of voice quality. In the first place, it has not been studied very widely or systematically, although there are certain notable exceptions. Secondly, because a particular voice quality is the result of life-long muscular habits, it is difficult to modify. And finally, because it is through general voice quality rather than the pronunciation of particular sounds that an individual is recognised, there is, in some learners, an in-built reluctance to change: voice quality, in that sense, is a hallmark of personality.

Motivation

Before attempting any description of the components of voice quality, the question of a learner's objectives and motivation needs to be considered. Many learners, on facing up to the realities of native-like voice quality and articulation – particularly in English – may decide that although they wish to speak English fluently, they neither want nor need to sound like a native speaker. They may wish to preserve some vestige of a foreign accent as a mark of their identity or nationality, and as a signal to the listener to 'make allowances'. Such learners should be treated in the same way as native speakers with a distinct regional accent: the accent is inseparable from the personality, and changing it also involves changing the image which the speaker presents to the world.

On the other hand, there are also many learners of foreign languages who very much want to sound native-like, or at least more authentic, but who do not know how to set about making the necessary general modifications to their pronunciation. It is this group of learners, many of whom may be the future teachers of languages, who have not been helped by the traditional approach to pronunciation teaching, and whose needs we should now aim to satisfy.

Components of voice quality

Abercrombie (1967:91) defines voice quality as 'those characteristics which are present more or less all the time that a person is talking: it is a quasi-permanent quality running through all the sound that issues from his mouth'. Viewed in this way voice quality would seem to be infinitely variable: there would be as many different voice qualities as there are individuals on the planet, and no way of isolating general or standardised components which could be taught or modified.

An alternative approach to the description of voice quality is to be found in Trudgill (1974). In describing the pronunciation of English speakers in the city of Norwich, he observes that 'the speech of many Norwich informants whose individual segments are otherwise quite or perhaps very similar actually sounds very different' (p. 185), and, elsewhere, that 'most of the components of the [Norwich] setting would appear to have little or no effect on the articulation of particular segments' (p. 187).

This suggests that even when a learner can produce individual sound segments which are very similar to those produced by a native speaker, they may still sound 'wrong' or 'foreign' because the overall voice quality is different. We ought, therefore, to look systematically for aspects of voice quality which are common to all speakers of a specified target variety, since even among native speakers (of different varieties) there may be important differences in quality.

For the remainder of this chapter we shall be concerned with the voice quality of the Southern British variety traditionally known as RP, and references to 'English' and 'English voice quality' should be interpreted as referring to this variety. The same approach could, of course, be applied to other standard varieties, such as General American.

We are concerned, therefore, not with features which enable us to recognise a particular individual's voice but with general characteristics which enable us to classify that voice as belonging to a native speaker of a particular language. In short, we are looking for an English stereotype which the learner can use as a target.

As has already been implied, a voice quality is the result of using the organs and muscles of phonation and articulation in a particular way. Our concern is therefore with describing the different parts of the articulatory apparatus and with classifying the different muscular activities which are employed in speaking. Since our main aim is to characterise the English voice, we shall also need to show the special use which English makes of the apparatus and to make broad comparisons with other languages.

The articulatory mechanism may conveniently be sub-divided into two major components: the *larynx*, where sound originates, and the *supralaryngeal tract* where it is shaped, modified and interrupted.

Use of the larynx

Unless the learner has studied singing, public speaking, or other modes of 'voice projection', it is unlikely that s/he will be aware of the variety of ways in which the larynx can be used. The physiology of the larynx and its associated muscles is complex and for our purposes it is necessary to reduce this to a small number of generalisations.

In its simplest terms the larynx may be raised, lowered or kept in a neutral position. English tends to keep the larynx in a neutral or slightly lowered position, whilst other languages make use of larger displacements. German and Italian, for example, tend to use a markedly lowered position, whilst Dutch and certain languages of Northern India make consistent use of a raised larynx. The auditory result of raising the larynx is a 'thin' or 'hard' and certainly less resonant sound, whereas lowering tends to give a 'warmer' and more resonant effect.

In addition, the larynx may be used with greater or less muscular energy, and with a higher or lower degree of tension. Thus one could say that English uses predominantly low energy and tension, whereas German uses higher energy and moderate tension (with a lowered larynx); Italian high energy and low tension (with a low larynx); and Dutch high energy and tension (with a raised larynx).

The perceptual result of this is that English sounds relatively relaxed and even 'breathy', while German and Italian sound more open and 'muscular', and Dutch rather 'constricted'. The problems of impressionistic labelling of this sort will be familiar to many teachers! (A fuller and more technical discussion of the classification of voice quality may be found in Laver, 1980, or Jenner, 1987.)

Above the larynx

The supralaryngeal tract may be stylised as a curved tube between the larynx and the lips. This tube may be of a fairly uniform cross-section or it may be habitually contricted at various points along its length. Thus a particular language may regularly use narrowing at the pharynx, or may keep some part of the tongue in a raised position. Alternatively the jaw may be open – to a greater or lesser extent – or kept in a raised or 'clenched' position. As with the larynx, these various activities may be performed with greater or lesser degrees of tension. Moreover, they all have important auditory effects which a listener (perhaps subconsciously) recognises and uses in the stereotyping of different accents.

It should be noted that we are not referring here to momentary closures, as in the case of particular stop consonants, but to the quasi-permanent shapes or 'settings' of particular languages. Some comparisons may again prove useful. Dutch, for example, has relatively high tension in the pharynx; German has raising of the front and centre of the tongue towards the palate; while English raises the tip of the tongue towards the teeth-ridge. As for the jaw, this is loosely closed in English, tensely half-open in Dutch, and energetically lowered and raised in Italian.

As a generalisation, one could say that the relaxation and lack of tension which are found in the English use of the larynx are also exhibited in the supralaryngeal tract, with the single exception of the tongue-tip. This is highly active in English, which results in an overall concave tongue shape and gives a secondary frontal or 'alveolar' quality to all English sounds, including so-called 'back' vowels. German has a predominantly palatal focus and sound quality, whilst in Dutch the predominant focus and sound quality is uvular.

More detailed discussion of these characteristics may again be found in Laver (1980). A comparison of the general features of English and Dutch is made in Jenner (1987), and a description of American English is provided in Esling and Wong (1983).

Summary

The general features which contribute to the quality of the English voice may conveniently be summarised as follows:

Laryngeal position:	neutral or slightly lowered
Laryngeal tension:	low
Supralaryngeal tract:	neutral and relaxed
	tongue-tip active
Jaw:	loosely closed
Lips:	lax
	slight rounding and spreading, but
	without tension

Teaching strategies

Since the modification of an acquired voice quality involves long-term and general adjustments to physical habits, it follows that it cannot be worked at piecemeal. The kind of vocal training involved depends to a very great extent on regular practice designed to develop the use of the vocal muscles in a particular way. In this sense it has more in common with the training of actors or singers than with traditional minimalist approaches to pronunciation teaching. And as with singing and acting success will depend on the learners' motivation and also on their ability to perceive and imagine the kind of sound which they wish to produce. The kind of exercises described below may be unfamiliar to most language teachers, although they fit well with such alternative approaches as Suggestopedia. They will also suit the kind of teaching which places a high value on the regular use of role play, caricature and other drama techniques.

Observation

1   The stiff upper lip

Using a video recording of a British newsreader or television announcer, with the sound turned off, students should be asked to observe and describe the facial movements employed in speaking English, concentrating on the very small movements which are used. Students will often comment that 'English speakers hardly move their mouths when they speak'. The stiff, or at least motionless, upper lip is a physical reality. If the teacher can also obtain a video recording of a speaker of French or Italian for contrast, this would be a good reinforcement.

2   The Andy Capp syndrome

This cartoon character frequently speaks with a cigarette between his lips. The teacher may also demonstrate that it is perfectly possible to speak English clearly with a pen-cap (if not a cigarette) or other lightweight object placed lightly (not gripped) between the lips. Students may then be encouraged to do the same, and should be reminded that it is usual in colloquial English to use no greater degree of openness than the thickness of a cigarette or pen-cap. It is, of course, possible to do this in any language, but in English it is the norm: any larger opening is reserved for public speaking or moments of great excitement.

3   *The larynx*

Students need to be sensitised to the mobility of the larynx. They may do this by placing a thumb and forefinger on either side of the 'Adam's apple', and then yawning and swallowing alternately. In yawning the larynx is pulled down from its rest position, while in swallowing it is pulled up.

In order to find an appropriate position for the larynx (neutral or slightly lowered), students will first have to establish what is the norm in their mother tongue and/or in their own idiolect.

If they normally use the larynx in a greatly lowered position, they may need advice on how to reduce this in speaking English. Here, speaking quietly, even whispering, or speaking at a slightly higher pitch may help, although it must be said that a lowered larynx will not in itself produce a particularly un-English sound, provided that it is not accompanied by great laryngeal tension. In this latter case, groaning or sighing on vowels may reduce the degree of vocal attack and excessive resonance, while whispering will draw attention to the flow of air through the larynx. This may then be combined with a gentle and breathy voicing to produce the relatively soft sound which characterises the English voice.

A raised larynx, however, is rather more of a problem, since it results in a hard sound (and possibly also a high pitch) found only in certain stigmatised native varieties which do not normally constitute a target for learners. Using the yawn mechanism and then voicing gently with a slightly lowered placement will show the student what is required. But regular physical practice will be needed before this becomes habitual.

The main characteristics to be cultivated in English laryngeal use are gentleness of attack and relatively fast airflow, since these will result in an approximation to a fairly neutral English stereotype.

Training

After observation of the operation of the vocal mechanism and the main characteristics of the English voice, the student is ready for a programme of exercises designed to develop some of the general features of English pronunciation. The aim of these exercises, it should be noted, is to develop habitual use of muscles in an English-like way. They are deliberately simple and global, so that the student may engage in useful self-directed practice away from the classroom. It should be noted that little attention is paid to the quality of individual sounds – particularly vowels – since native speech shows considerable idiosyncratic variation at the segmental level.

Certain types of individual sound are used in exercises, but only where they will help to develop a general feature such as aspiration or laxity. The fundamental principle, however, is that if a native-like framework or 'setting' can be achieved, all that happens within it will also be perceived as native-like.

1   *Relaxation*

Since the salient characteristic of the English voice is laxity, it is vital to develop a whole-body approach to relaxation. This is achieved through breathing exercises. Teachers familiar with yoga may wish to use the sort of breathing cycle which opens and closes a sequence of yoga exercises. This involves lying on the floor in the 'corpse' position, with the feet slightly apart and the hands (palms upwards) a few inches from the hips. As an in-breath is taken the abdomen rises, and it falls as the breath is expelled. On each in-breath one limb is tensed, and then released on the out-breath. Attention is drawn to possible hidden tensions in the shoulders, neck, lips, tongue, fingers and toes.

Breathing is slow:

in	to a count of 2
hold	to a count of 4
out	to a count of 4

The in-breath should simulate a yawn, and the out-breath a gentle sigh.

Many teaching spaces, of course, do not have sufficient room for students to recline comfortably on the floor. Moreover, teachers not versed in yoga may not feel comfortable in handling breathing exercises in this way. In such circumstances the same sort of routine can be carried out in a sitting position. Ideally, the students should have room to sit back, preferably in high-backed armless chairs, with the head supported, arms hanging loose and legs extended comfortably forward.

Again, the same cycle of tensing on the in-breath, holding, and then relaxing on the out-breath is followed, with particular attention to the rise and fall of the abdomen and to forgotten tensions in shoulders, neck, tongue and lips.

The purpose of this breathing cycle, which needs to be carried out daily, is to free the body from the habitual tensions associated with the mother-tongue and to prepare it to engage in the 'new' activities of English. It also has the advantage of stilling the mind, flooding the brain with oxygen and putting the student into an ideal state of receptivity for all kinds of learning. Since the English voice requires almost total laxity, the student who does no more than learn to relax fully will go a considerable way towards achieving an authentic English-like sound.

2 *The tongue*

Within this totally relaxed framework, one part of the articulatory mechanism is extremely active in English: the tip of the tongue. Cine-radiography of English speech shows clearly the kind of focused pecking movement made by the tongue-tip on or towards the teeth-ridge. In practising this, however, the learner needs to be reminded of two things: (*i*) any closure made by the tongue is comparatively gentle and without undue pressure; and (*ii*) the breath-flow for English should be maintained as long as possible, and even allowed to leak a little around voiceless stops, so that a typically aspirated release can be achieved.

The regular practice of a number of rhythmic sentences with frequent /t/ sounds will assist the development of these features:

> *Take these tins to the tip.*
> *A ten-ton truck was attempting to turn.*

(Teachers may care to invent more of their own examples.) To achieve the right degree of relaxation and aspiration it is preferable that the sentences should be spoken quietly, and preferably whispered initially. Many students will, moreover, need to be reminded frequently to use the tongue-tip only, rather than a larger area. They should also be asked to find and stroke the teeth-ridge with the tongue-tip before even attempting to articulate.

3 *The lips*

The aspiration and lax closure which apply to the use of the tongue are also characteristic of English usage of the lips. Before any consonantal exercises are attempted, therefore, the students should practise simply blowing through slack lips to produce a repeated 'pf', or popping sound, of the sort that young children make. Then, a repertoire of short sentences with a high frequency of voiceless initial /p/-sounds may be practised and committed to memory:

> *Put your pen in the appropriate place.*
> *A push-pull process gives powerful pressure.*

4 *Vowel length*

English vowels make very distinct length contrasts. That is to say, English long vowels are extremely long, and short vowels very short. The long vowels may be directly linked to muscular laxity, since the kind of drawled vowels characteristic of British (and also, incidentally, American) English can only be achieved if the overall setting is free from tension. This laxity has one further result in the pronunciation of English long vowels: all long vowels – not only diphthongs – have a tendency to glide to a more central position rather than to remain in a stable or 'pure' position.

Again this should be related to relaxation and exercises devised which exaggerate the length of vowels:

> *Try to buy tea.*
> *High as an elephant's eye.*
> *The boy will go away.*

These, and other words ending in long open vowels or diphthongs, will enable students to practise extending the length of vowels far beyond what they believe to be necessary.

Achieving appropriate vowel-length, incidentally, has the added benefit that it facilitates the kind of gliding pitch-movements which characterise English intonation.

Further sources

Once the teacher has become familiar with the type of exercises needed to develop the general features of the English voice, it becomes relatively easy to create more practice activities along the same lines or to select from conventional pronunciation manuals those exercises which will encourage this kind of general articulatory development. Other suitable material may be found in the following books and articles:

Baker, A. (1982) *Introducing English Pronunciation* Cambridge University Press.
Esling, J.H. (1987) 'Methodology for voice setting awareness in language classes' in *Revue de Phonétique Appliquée* (Mons) 85:449–473.
Jenner, B. and Bradford, B. (1982) 'Is your tongue right?' in *Modern English Teacher* 10:2.
Van Lysebeth, A. (1971) *Yoga Self-taught* Unwin, London.
McCallion, M. (1988) *The Voice Book* Faber, London.
Wessels, C. (1982) *Drama* Oxford University Press.

References

Abercrombie, D. (1967) *Elements of General Phonetics* Edinburgh University Press.
Arnold, R. and Hansen, K. (1979) *Englische Phonetik* VEB Leipzig.
Esling, J.H. and Wong, R. (1983) 'Voice quality settings and the teaching of pronunciation' in *TESOL Quarterly* 17:89–95.
Honikman, B. (1964) 'Articulatory settings' in *In Honour of Daniel Jones* (eds. D. Abercrombie *et al.*) Longman, London.
Jenner, B. (1987) 'Articulation and phonation in non-native English' in *Journal of the International Phonetic Association* 17:2.
Laver, J. (1980) *The Phonetic Description of Voice Quality* Cambridge University Press.
Trudgill, P. (1974) *The Social Differentiation of English in Norwich* Cambridge University Press.

Chapter 5
Rhymes and Rhythm

Michael Vaughan-Rees
Eurocentre Lee Green

Introduction

Parents, the world over, teach verses and songs to their children which they, in their turn, pass on to their own children. Schoolchildren acquire a different set of songs, rhymes and chants, this time from older children or teachers. Thinking back to my own childhood I can summon them forth in their dozens:

Hickory dickory dock, the mouse ran up the clock . . .

Round and round the garden, like a teddy bear,
one step, two step, tickle you under there.

Eeeny, meeny, miney, mo, catch a tinker by the toe . . .

I'm the king of the castle and you're the dirty rascal.

Remember, remember the Fifth of November . . .

In fourteen hundred and ninety-two,
Columbus sailed the ocean blue.

Why is it that I am absolutely word-perfect when it comes to sequences like these but would find it difficult to reproduce anything said to me in prose 40 minutes (let alone 40 years) ago? It may well be that much of the verse was repeated, possibly dozens of times. But it may have something to do with the inherent memorability of verse, especially when allied to a strong, rhythmic beat. Our first sensation, after all, is surely the beat of our mother's heart, a beat echoed in the comforting movement used to lull us to sleep as babies, and reproduced in the lullabies which are the first examples of verse to which most of us are exposed.

Wise language teachers, whatever the language, take advantage of the universal appeal of rhyme and rhythm. For those teaching English, however, it is especially to be recommended, since English is likely to be considerably more rhythmic than the L1 of their students. And the unit of rhythm in English is the *stressed syllable* rather than the syllable itself.

Names

I like to demonstrate this point by using names, since names, by their very nature, cause few problems of meaning and hence are suitable even at beginners' level. One technique is to have a series of individual names prepared in such a way that they can be moved around (using OHP, pinboard or magnet board). The class should imagine that they are at a party and are introducing three friends to the gathering. Start with names consisting of just one syllable and demonstrate the regular beat by saying, for example,

         o   o   o
    This is Tim, Sue an(d) Mark.

Next replace one of the above by a two-syllable name (such as *Andrew*, *Mary*, *Dianne* or *Peter*) and show that the beat remains the same, wherever the longer name goes. Then show how the same thing happens even when a three-syllable name is included and whatever the order. Thus:

              o   o   o
    This is Amanda, Tim and Andrew.
    This is Andrew, Tim and Amanda
    This is Amanda, Andrew and Tim.

A good follow-up is to divide the class into groups of three and tell them to choose English first names for themselves, one of one syllable, one of two and one of three or more. They then take turns in saying the following introduction:

    Hello, I'm (name) and this is (name) and (name).

The choosing of names makes them think about how many syllables there actually are in words such as *Margaret* (two) and *Catherine* (two or three). And in order for them to keep to the beat they have not only to hit the stressed syllables, but to distinguish between vowels of varying length. They have, in particular, to avoid giving undue emphasis to the very weak syllables found in many names, especially those of three or more syllables. You should also encourage them to make appropriate links as well as to produce the weak form of *and*, possibly with elision of the final /d/.

    Hello, I'm Andrew an(d) this is Peter and Anne.

Place names, too, are useful for demonstrating the contrast between stressed and unstressed syllables, particularly where what originally were lexical items (such as *home*, *ford* and *town*) have become reduced to weak, unstressed suffixes. Here is part of a simple poem I wrote, linking personal and place names by the use of identical first sounds. The rhyme scheme is AABC DDBC and the beat is a simple ONE two three, ONE two three.[1]

> o   o
> Norman's from Nottingham,
> Martin's from Mottingham,
> Charley's from Chester
> and Lesley's from Lee.
>
> Joyce is from Jarrow
> and Henry's from Harrow,
> Laura's from Leicester
> and Dave's from Dundee.
>
> Ed comes from Eltham
> and Fred comes from Feltham,
> Brian's from Braintree
> and Chris comes from Crewe.
>
> Colin's from Kerry
> and Bobby's from Bury,
> Ada's from Aintree
> So, how about you?

This also reinforces the troublesome pronunciation of certain place names, e.g. *Leicester* is two syllables, and rhymes with *Chester*, similarly *Bury* with *Kerry*.

Students can be asked to fill in extra verses using the following pairs of towns: *Stratford/Catford*; *Stainton/Paignton*; *Cork/York*; *Goole/Poole*; *Carlisle/Argyll*; *Fawley/Crawley*; *Hull/Mull*; *Tenby/Denbigh*; *Taunton/Staunton*; *Marlow/Harlow*; *Ware/Kildare*; *Bolton/South Molton*.

Do-it-yourself tongue-twister kit[2]

This combination of alliteration and rhythm is also found in my 'Do-it-yourself tongue-twister kit' which starts at a fairly elementary level, with various additions taking it gradually up to advanced level.

1   Start by writing up three sentences such as

Kenneth bought some cabbage.
Peter bought some peanuts.
Brenda bought some bread.

Tell the class that you are asking about the *sound* of the sentences and not their *spelling*. Read them aloud and ask what they have in common. If someone says that the rhythm is the same, then that is fine; get the class to say them in chorus, with heavy stress on name and product. But ask what else they have in common. The class may need some prompting, but eventually someone will catch on to the fact that the initial sounds are the same (alliteration). Then concentrate on the name/product pairs and ask how they differ. This time, you may have to point out that *Kenneth* and *cabbage* have just one initial sound in common, *Peter* and *peanuts* have two, while *Brenda* and *bread* have three.

Next divide the class into groups and, if possible, allocate enough board space for each to write up a series of name and product pairs. At the lowest level it can be anything buyable; higher up insist on something to eat or drink. Tell them that a *Kenneth/cabbage* type choice gives one point, *Peter/peanuts* two points and so on, and that no repetition is allowed. Then give them three or four minutes to write up as many as possible. The teacher's task is to shout out if she sees anyone writing a word which has already been used and rub out the example.

Now comes the real ear-training. Each group has to state how many points it deserves for a given pair but gets none at all if the wrong choice is made. Expecting two points for *Susan/sugar* and three points for *Tom/tomatoes* are typical examples of unjustified claims.

2   The next stage is to write examples of sequences such as the following:

o	o	o	o
Katherine	bought	a kilo	of cabbage
Paula	bought	a pocketful	of peanuts
Gerry	bought	a jar	of jam
Rudolph	bought	a room full	of radishes.

Elicit further examples – this is perhaps best done for homework. Then, to demonstrate that each sequence can be said with the same rhythm, I have the class chant another one of my doggerel poems (quite fast, with claps or finger clicks on the off beat).

o	o	o	o
Arthur	bought (pause)	an armful	of artichokes,
Belinda	bought	a barrelful	of beans,
Catherine	bought	a kilo	of cabbages, and
Sandra	bought	a sack	of sardines.

Peter	bought	a pocketful	of peanuts,
Queenie	bought	a quarter pound	quince,
Shirley	bought	a shop full	of sugar lumps, and
Michael	bought	a milligram	of mince.

Cuthbert	bought	a cupful	of custard,
Brenda	bought	a bucketful	of bream,
Muriel	bought	a mugful	of mustard, and
Christopher	bought	a crateful	of cream.

3   Now go on to replace *bought* by another verb. The choice can be as wild as you like, provided that the rule of alliteration is kept to (though by now it is difficult to have more than the initial sound in common).

4   Finally you add an adjective to the name, to produce sequences such as the following:

> Artful Arthur argued for an armful of artichokes.
> Able Amos ached for an acre of apricots.
> Cheerful Charlie chose a chewy chunk of chocolate.
> Fragrant Freda fried a fridge full of fritters.
> Flighty Flossie flaunted a flat full of flapjacks.
> Lofty Lawrence longed for a lorry-load of lobsters.
> Naughty Norman gnawed a knob of nutty nougat.
> Posh Patricia purchased a pound of Polish peaches.
> Sly Salome sliced a sliver of salami.
> Tiny Tina tasted a teaspoonful of tuna.
> Vicious Victor vanished in a vat full of vanilla.
> Weary Wanda waded in a waggon load of water-cress.

The end result is a set of friendly tongue-twisters, which the students have had a hand in producing. And at each stage you have a series of utterances which can be read out using the same rhythmic beat.

Limericks

It is more usual, of course, to practise the rhythm of English by using ready-made verse and songs. One problem with this is that the syllables which are stressed in verse and song are not necessarily those which would be stressed in natural speech. Referring to an article by Scholey (1986) called 'There was an old man of Calcutta', Adam Brown has demonstrated that limericks, especially, may be misleading in this respect. In the line which forms the title of Scholey's article the stress falls on *was, man* and *Calcutta* whereas in natural speech, 'the stresses would be placed differently – on *old, man* and *Calcutta*. In particular, it would be very unusual for the verb *was* to be stressed, as this would imply you were contradicting a previous insinuation such as "I don't think there was any old man".' (Brown, 1990)

But not all limericks start with *There was a . . .* Provided that the traditional metre and rhyme scheme are kept to, then anything goes. And it is one of the easiest verse forms to write. Here are three of my own.

> *A student from sunny Algiers*
> *would frequently burst into tears,*
> *for her rhythm and stress*
> *were a terrible mess,*
> *and yet she'd been trying for years!*

Another from Lima (Peru)
said 'Teacher, just what should I do?
Does "cough" rhyme with "rough"
and "bough" with "enough",
and what about "thorough" and "through"?'

Another young student from Spain
said 'Teacher, please could you explain
why "bury" and "ban"
and "very" and "van"
are different? To me they're the same!!'

Raps

Raps, like limericks, often exhibit a cavalier attitude towards stress placement. I have tried to avoid that problem in the following poem, which was devised in order to practice a wide range of features associated with informal speech: linking, weak forms, elision and coalescent assimilation. The use of non-standard written forms to indicate features of casual speech is borrowed from Weinstein (1988).

WHERE DJA WANNA GO?

A. *Where dja wanna go,*   (Where do you want to go?)
    whatcha wanna do?   (What do you want to do?)

B. *I'm no' too sure,*   (I'm not too sure)
    I leave it ta you.   (I'll leave it to you)

A. *Doncha wanna go*   (Don't you want to go
    ta see a show?   to see a show?)

B. *I don' know now*   (I don't know now
    but I letcha know   but I'll let you know)

A. *Didja tell the others*   (Did you tell . . .)
    where we're gointa meet?   (we're going to . . .)

B. *I said in the centre,*
    didn' say which street.   (didn't say . . .)

A. *Dja wanna have a meal or*   (do you want to . . .)
    dja like ta sit down?   (would you like to . . .)

B. *Dja fancy eating first*   (Do you fancy . . .)
    in Chinatown?

A. *Whatcha recommend?*   (What do you . . .)
    Wheredja like ta dine?   (Where would you like to . . .)

B. *Here's very good,*
    their fish is fine.

A. *Howdja like the meal,*   (How did you . . .)
    Didja like the fish?   (Did you like . . .)

B. *It was really great,*
   what's the namea the dish?   (name of the dish)

A. *I don' know the name,*   (I don't know ...)
   it wasn' written down.   (it wasn't written ...)

B. *That's often the way*
   ... in Chinatown.

Poems

Many teachers have been successful in encouraging students to produce their own poetry. But it is probably not a good idea to start with that most daunting of things, a blank page. It is best perhaps to present them with existing material in some sort of incomplete or unacceptable form. Lines may be presented in the wrong order and groups of students compete to reassemble them. Or the conventions may be broken. Here, for example, is a distorted version of one of my limericks.

> *A student from Algiers*
> *would frequently burst into tears.*
> *For her intonation and stress*
> *were a terrible mess,*
> *and yet she'd been trying for a very long time!*

In this case the students (who should already be familiar with the form) would see who can come up with an acceptable version.

Perhaps the simplest method is to give out poems with various words (or longer sequences) missing. The degree of difficulty can be controlled by (*a*) the choice of poem; (*b*) the number, nature and positioning of words omitted; (*c*) the decision whether or not to provide a jumbled list of missing words (and if so, whether to include some distractors). Try to fill in the gaps in the following poem (written as a follow-up to the *Kenneth bought some cabbage* sequence). The missing words are listed in Footnote 3.

> GOING SHOPPING
> *Every time she goes out shopping*
> *Mary Williams drives a whopping*
> *great big ... (1) ... just to carry all she ... (2) ...*
>
> *For her family's so ... (3) ...*
> *that she really needs a barge*
> *(there are twenty-four of every ... (4) ... and size).*
>
> *As she drives her lorry ... (5) ...*
> *to the centre of the ... (6) ...*
> *all the tradesmen start to ... (7) ... and cheer and ... (8) ...*
>
> *For she spends vast sums of ... (9) ...*
> *just on bread and jam and honey*
> *(not to mention all the wine and beer and stout).*

> *And ... (10) ... day she buys ... (11) ...*
> *(that's for Margaret, Fred and Betty)*
> *and some mutton chops with very little fat.*
>
> *And a metre of baloney*
> *with a ... (12) ... of macaroni*
> *and a ... (13) ... of something tasty for the ... (14) ...*
>
> *As for her, what ... (15) ... she eat,*
> *is it fish or fruit or ... (16) ...?*
> *What's the kind of thing that mothers like the best?*
>
> *Well she's got no ... (17) ... for eating*
> *for she's cooking or she's ... (18) ...*
> *up the food she's bought to serve to all the rest.*

With a class I would read the poem through (without their seeing it), make them aware of the rhyme and metre scheme, then give out the text and have them work in groups to provide words to fit the gaps. You will see that choices are governed by a specific set of constraints. Firstly, all the words have to make sense in the context; those within lines have in addition to fit the metre; finally, those at line endings have to fit both metre and rhyme scheme. Look at the clues which guide our choice in the first stanza, for example. They are:

1 *Grammatical.* We know that (1) must be a singular noun as it follows *a* and that (2) must be a verb with an -*s* ending.
2 *Semantic.* (1), since it collocates with *drive*, must be part of the set which includes *car/van/lorry/truck/tank/train* etc.
3 *Phonological.* The metre makes it likely that (1) will fit the stress pattern O o, thus excluding every member of the set except *lorry* (which is also more appropriate in terms of *lorry/carry* alliteration). And (2) must be a monosyllabic rhyme for *size*.

Care is needed in dealing with inappropriate choices, though, since some are less impossible than others. The following choice fits the grammatical and semantic criteria, but it would mean cramming one syllable too many into the first line.

> *And **every** day she buys spaghetti*
> *(that's for Margaret, Fred and Betty)*

If you notice a student writing *every*, commend them for making sense, but get them to read it aloud. If they do not see the point, ask them to find a one-syllable word which can replace *every* (or supply it, if necessary).

In fact, having the students read aloud is, in my opinion, very important. Furthermore, it is worth training them to do so with some degree of skill. Leave them on their own and, in the case of this particular poem, they are likely, for example, to give similar emphasis to both the opening lines, as if a *whopping* was an unusual make of car.

Every time she goes out shopping
Mary Williams drives a whopping.

Demonstrate that there is no pause, fall–rise or whatever at a line ending unless it corresponds to a boundary between syntactic units. That is, indeed, the case with line 1, whereas the unit initiated in line 2 is *a whopping great big lorry*. Not only that; your students should be trained to vary the emphasis of words according to their degree of importance, novelty, or predictability.

For her family's so large
that she really needs a barge.

In the above couplet it is clear that *large* and *barge* should be more prominent than the surrounding words. *Barge*, moreover, should not only be most prominent of all, it should further contrast with *large* in terms of intonation. *Large*, dealing, as it does with information already given – the size of the family – should be said with a fall–rise; *barge*, on the other hand, should be said with high fall, in view of its status as a unit of new information.

Conclusion

Ah, you may say; why, near the end of an article about rhymes and rhythm, are we starting to talk about intonation? But the various components of speech are interdependent; and a feel for the rhythm of English (subsuming, as it does, an awareness of stress) would seem to be a prerequisite for control of the intonation system.

But leaving that aside, there seems little point in training students to drone out poems with impeccable feel for metre yet with no evidence of understanding. Poetry, after all, is an enhanced form of regular spoken language. And if learners of English begin to read poems with something approaching the realities of speech, then, in my opinion, their actual spoken pronunciation can only benefit.

Notes

1 The poems quoted in this chapter have all been shortened. The complete versions of these (and of other poems, raps, chants etc.) are to be found in *Speak Out!* 8, the special *Rhymes & Rhythm* issue of the Newsletter of the IATEFL Phonology Special Interest Group (ed. Michael Vaughan-Rees, 1991). The copyright of the poems in this chapter is retained by Michael Vaughan-Rees.
2 The term 'Do-it-yourself' is borrowed from David Orme, editor of the excellent magazine *Creative Language*, who has written *The D.I.Y. Poetry Book*, which Collins are due to publish in 1992.
3 Here are the missing words: (1) lorry, (2) buys, (3) large, (4) shape, (5) down, (6) town, (7) jump (laugh, smile, wave etc.), (8) shout, (9) money, (10) each, (11)

spaghetti, (12) sack (pack, ton etc.), (13) tin (can, bit etc.), (14) cat, (15) does, (16) meat, (17) time, (18) heating.

References

Brown, A. (1990) 'Some caveats about using pop songs' in *Speak Out!* (Newsletter of the IATEFL Phonology Special Interest Group) 7:3–8.
Scholey, M. (1986) 'There was an old man of Calcutta', *Modern English Teacher*, 13(3):22–26.
Weinstein, N. (1988) *Whaddaya Say?* Prentice-Hall, New Jersey.

Chapter 6
Sentence Stress – For More Meaningful Speech

Brita Haycraft
International House, London

Introduction

Sentence stress is like a backbone. Without it, the utterance is vague and shapeless. Children communicate via sentence stress before learning to say the words properly.

Of all the pronunciation skills to give to learners, sentence stress is probably the most valuable, as it quickly helps them communicate effectively, even with very little English. Without it, students merely line up words. With it, they make sense.

There are many interesting aspects of English sentence stress. In this chapter I will focus on those which seem most relevant to learners and their teachers, and are easy to apply in the students' classroom preparation for outside conversations.

Sentence stress may be observed from two angles:

1   As it appears in speech – the finished product as it were, the stresses occurring at intervals, the intervening words shortened, even contracted.
2   From the speaker's point of view, watching how he/she manoeuvres stress and why.

The latter approach has more in it for the learner, who can only gain from identifying with the speaker and getting to know some useful speaker tactics. Similarly, I feel that it is better for the learner to spend more time on production (speaking) than on reception (listening), as actually using stress also leads to noticing stress and to better understanding.

The common term *sentence stress* is used in this chapter, in place of the lesser-known but more appropriate *utterance stress*, that is, the stress in a single utterance with only one sentence clause.

There are two other aspects of sentence stress with which this chapter does not deal. For the sake of the learner, only main stresses

It is possible that teachers-to-be only need to know the following rule: when speaking, we normally only stress the words that are important to us, in the given context. Perhaps learners only need to be told the following: when you speak, remember to stress only the words that are important to you in the context (as doubtless you do in your own languages). This advice works well, as long as secondary stresses are regarded as unstressed.

Some readers may wonder about the place of fluency, rhythm and the ebb and flow of the sentence – essential realities of speech. The answer is, I think, that foreign students can only begin to speak more rhythmically, on their own, when they know which words to stress, and that is the skill or awareness they first need to learn.

Many books state that we normally stress words like nouns, verbs and adjectives. Naturally, content words like *country, ship* and *love* with their rich meanings are important in terms of information, and are therefore likely to get stressed more often than insignificant grammar works like *a, of* and *than*. Frequently, though, content words play a minor role in the context, and the speaker indicates this by a reduction in stress:

This is my cup and that's your cup

Sentence stress changes from an abstract area into a useful speaking tool when students realise it is they, as speakers, who decide which words to stress. Here are two examples of types of exchange. In the first type, the speaker responds, directly connecting stress with the main point of the context given by A's line:

1　A:　What time is it?
　　B:　It is half past.

　　A:　Is it twenty past?
　　B:　No, it is half past.

　　A:　See you at half past.
　　B:　It is half past.

But in the second, the speaker responds, at the same time inserting an additional idea, which overrules the obvious stress connection:

2　A:　What time is it?
　　B:　It is half past.
　　　　(The speaker also reveals she thought it was perhaps twenty past.)

or　B:　It is half past.
　　　　(Perhaps the speaker had hoped it was not yet half past.)

Stress is never haphazard. There is a system and the speaker is in charge of it. The indirect use of stress in example 2 above may sound devious but it does have its reasons, even if they are well hidden.

Coming from a foreign speaker, it would probably be a mistake and sound like one. But as with intricate grammar or vocabulary points, this is one of those finer aspects of language to be studied at advanced level, if at all. The use of stress in example 1, meanwhile, with the obvious stress connections, is of great value to learners, making them flexible with stress, and enabling them to express different meanings without having to change the words.

Students who use stress in the right way speak English better. In the first place it shows they heard and understood the question. For example, it is impressive when in reply to 'Can you come at a quarter past two?', a student answers 'I can come at <u>half</u> past two' instead of scatty-sounding answers like 'I can come at half <u>past</u> two' or 'I <u>can</u> come at half past <u>two</u>' which hold out little hope for proper communication. The sooner students get into the habit of actively *using* stress, in different places, the better for everyone.

Students' problems

Students not initiated in the use of stress often remain oblivious of its function and sadly produce a kind of 'robotspeak' even at an advanced level:

He asked <u>me</u> so I told <u>him</u> that there <u>was</u> nothing in <u>it</u>.

Personality and smiles may compensate but only in face-to-face situations. Over the telephone, intercom and radio, for instance, the stress needs to be in the right place. This is important for professional groups such as hotel staff and aircraft crew. It is also of course required of foreign teachers of English.

Yet, if provoked into contradicting, foreign learners seem to employ stress in much the same definite way as native English speakers, which shows that it is a familiar concept. Even so, the learners usually ignore stress, placing it arbitrarily without much relation to the context. The reason is probably the learner situation itself: struggling with grammar and words just makes them forget about stress. Or focusing on particular words, they stress them inappropriately. Occasionally, the wrong word stress can upset the sentence stress. People are not normally conscious of using stress anyway, so why expect it from learners stumbling along in a foreign language?

An added complication is the students' tendency not to contract unstressed words, with the result that these sound stressed to a native English ear and blur the important part of the message. This failure to contract can accidentally make students sound pedantic, when using the strong form instead of the weak one:

I did not <u>see</u> it.
instead of   I didn't <u>see</u> it.

are considered, all other words with secondary or lesser stress being treated as unstressed. The aim is to prevent students from overstressing unimportant words. This chapter also does not cover the unstressed contracted words known as *weak forms*, except to say that the firmer the students' grasp of the stressed words, the better their chances of weakening the unstressed words as customary.

The physical features of stress

Stress is a voice effort made on a particular word (or syllable) in various noticeable ways: the stressed syllable seems louder, or it makes a jump in the intonation, or it gets slightly prolonged, as sometimes detected in whispered speech. Other elements enter in, too, like tiny pauses and a sensation of force or pressure. This is presumably how stress is noted in any language and so is nothing a foreign student needs to learn anew. The only advantage of knowing the actual mechanics is when you need to check if a syllable is stressed or not in a recording for the purposes of speech research or clandestine listening, perhaps.

Noticing stress

Native English listeners notice stress in a variety of ways, even indirectly via its very absence on words, particularly if those words are drastically contracted. Foreign learners cannot be expected to rely on the contractions. They have to listen for the stresses.

I find that, unless distracted by some language detail, students have little difficulty hearing the stressed words, and still less when asked to link stress to the important words. In theory, the contracted unstressed words should make the stresses stand out more clearly to the learner's ear. But it takes a little time for the foreign learner to get used to the 'disappearing act' of the weak forms.

Native English listeners, on the contrary, are used to contracted syllables, and can find it difficult to hear stresses in another language when the unstressed vowel sounds are not contracted.

Producing stress

When it comes to speaking, the only problem is knowing which words to stress. A common sense way of deciding is to weigh up the text and the context, and conclude which word or words deserve stress:

> (In a cafeteria) I'd like a <u>sandwich</u>, please.

Obviously *sandwich* is the most important word here, also shown as the speaker cuts it down to simply 'A <u>sandwich</u>, please'.

You /mʌs/ turn <u>left</u> here.
instead of   You /məs/ turn <u>left</u> here.

It would not help if the concept of stress were presented as being specific to English. In fact it could cause confusion as it is doubtful if stressless languages exist. The fact that words are not contracted does not mean that there are no stresses. The main stress in 'This is <u>my</u> handbag' is perfectly clear even though the vowel sounds are fully pronounced. there would be little point in speaking if none of the words was significant. Nor can one imagine every word having the same importance in the context all the time.

Where English does differ is in the extent to which stress is used, the speaker constantly moving it to emphasise a new point without a change of words. This is good news for learners as they too can move stress about, communicating more subtly without learning any new words. The bad news is that they also have to start contracting unstressed words.

On the whole, students respond well to the notion of stress and we do not need to spend too long explaining the system. Teaching becomes more a matter of reminding students to use stress in the new language too.

Training the learners

There are numerous techniques that activate the sentence stress. They should be quick and unobtrusive so as to fit into the general language work, not just to give the wobbly grammar practice some shape, but also to show the students how stress helps them. It increases their understanding, improves their communication, and adds a glimmer of life.

Here are various easy techniques, tricks and strategies, presented in the order in which they may be needed.

The contradiction principle

This is an easy technique that goes with any classroom practice. Basically the teacher provokes an answer by asking false questions, that is, 'no'-questions rather than 'yes'-questions:

   T: (knowing the real answer is Africa): Did he go to America?
   S: No, he went to <u>Africa</u>.

Because this is a much easier question to answer than a general *wh*-question, the student answers more spontaneously with clear well-placed stress.

Should the stress get stuck on *went*, the student worrying about the past tense form, you can go on 'misunderstanding', using false statements too:

> T: I see, he went to America.
> or   Did he like America?
> or   How long was he in America?

Thus pushed, the student does eventually move the stress into place. This sort of gentle teasing also speeds up the saying of complex grammar structures, as in this situation where students say what they would have done, had they found some money in the street:

> T: So, you'd have left the £20 note in the street?
> S: No, I'd have picked it up.

The questions should be without any give-away stress and students are better off avoiding the short answer 'I wouldn't' after 'No'.

Suggesting a context

A practice sentence on its own on the board is open to a number of stress possibilities:

> I usually have tea for breakfast.

But with a prompt question and a hinted context in a two-line dialogue, the stresses emerge and the whole item is easier to practise:

> T: What do you have for breakfast?
> or   Do you have coffee for breakfast?
>
> S: I usually have tea.
> or   I usually have tea for breakfast.

A conversational setting also produces more natural exchanges and gets rid of superfluous words put there merely to practise more grammar.

Awareness of stress

With a new class, the teacher can begin by correcting the stress in the students' spoken practice. Soon, however, it is time to consolidate a few points.

An ordinary practice sentence is written up on the board: 'Where do you live?' Asked what the most important words are, the students soon figure it out: *where* and *live*. Then the stress is marked in some noticeable way.

The term *stress* might as well be used from the start, describing it as 'the strong words' or 'putting the emphasis on the important or interesting words, in this situation'. With beginners, simply translate it if possible. Later, I like asking which words the students *want* to stress in a given sentence, as a reminder that it is up to them to decide. It is a good idea to repeat the sentence a few times with the students listening to the stresses, but it is important they also have a chance to *say* the sentence with the indicated stress. If necessary, the teacher can offer two different positions and let the students compare them: 'Is it <u>last</u> week or last <u>week</u>?' Once students get the practice sentence right with the stresses <u>in</u> place, it makes all the difference if they say it again a bit faster and more naturally, savouring the stresses and absorbing the contractions. This improves the whole speech flow.

'Telegramspeak'

A good way of shaping the sentence is to let the students do a sort of 'telegramspeak', saying only the stressed syllables but keeping the appropriate attitude and pauses for the left out words:

<u>How</u> much is that   black <u>umbrella</u>?
<u>How</u>....................... black . brell?

Do you   <u>mind</u> if I have a   <u>look</u>   at your <u>camera</u>?
.... mind ....   look................... cam....?

Although it is effective and fun, there is no need to treat every practice sentence that way. The stresses can be used as invaluable support especially for longer sentences, like pegs on which to hang the sentence, or stepping stones in the torrent of speech, enabling the students to advance more quickly and confidently. They certainly also make useful crutches for anyone wanting to rehearse a speech. A visual link between the words also helps speed up the speaking: 'Do you mind if I have a look at your camera?'

Correction work

Correction should be quick and simple. Most students are able to correct their stress mistakes, through imitation or reasoning. The teacher may want to reinforce the place of stress with a (silent) simultaneous hand movement.

I used to favour beating the stress with hand movements like a conductor. This sometimes works with large groups, as long as the natural contextual stress is not lost. In an ordinary class I prefer to sort it out from the context in the spirit of lively rehearsal by the students rather than a drill.

If a student really cannot get the stress right, the teacher can either leave it, or try to solve it by also getting the student to make a gentle hand or head movement. An accompanying physical movement some-times does the trick. A colleague of mine tries having his students raise their eyebrows as they stress the word, though you need to know your students well for this. Tapping or clapping, however, makes it difficult to hear the words and can be a bit elaborate for ordinary language practice. Whispering the sentence can also sometimes put the stress right, as the stressed syllables get lengthened and the vowels are subdued, and the fact that students have no objection to whispering.

The role of homework must not be underestimated. If the stresses are marked in a sentence, students can easily practise saying it at home and experiment with stress on different words. With a cassette player, they can also do various discovery tasks and self dictations (see below).

Students are bound to get better at sentence stress if the teacher gets into the habit of praising them for trying, even if the grammar is still faulty. Given time and special classes, all sorts of techniques could be tried out. But if sentence stress plays an active part in the general language lesson, this straightforward skill does not need special practice.

Listening practice

When a tape is played in class for comprehension or language presentation, it is worth pausing now and again to ask the students to repeat the stressed words they heard. This is not only to make the class more lively or to practise stress *per se*, but also to help the students get an idea of what the passage is about, since the stresses correspond with the main points of the dialogue or story. Once a regular practice, it is a valid alternative to comprehension questions, students giving the gist on the basis of the stresses. This sharpens their ear and makes them more confident they can understand spoken English without having to see the people or the text.

The sentence stress can act as a clue to a story. Listening to a passage, students write down the words with the most stress and from that they get an idea of the action: 'Once ... time ... girl ... Red Riding ...' This can be developed further, the students writing down the stresses as a form of note-taking. When more used to it, students can listen for the stresses *before* the vocabulary is explained, practising for more authentic situations.

Once they realise they can partly depend on the stresses for meaning, they may be more willing to listen to the radio or to see a play rather than a musical at the theatre. It is a matter of starting stress spotting on a small scale and letting it develop into a habit. The listening activity should not be entirely passive, however. It also thrives on the occasional loud repetition and sampling of the sentences so carefully listened to.

Predicting stress

The idea of predicting the stresses in a dialogue can be introduced early on. The students read the dialogue due to be played and decide which words are likely to be stressed. Then as the teacher plays the dialogue, they check if they were right or wrong. Most of the time they get it right, which boosts their confidence, especially when they pick up subtleties. In the following dialogue (from *Streamline Departures*), students may think *wine* is stressed every time, until they take the context into account:

Customer: Oh, and I'd like some <u>wine</u>.
Waiter: <u>Which</u> wine would you <u>like</u>, sir?
Customer: A <u>bottle</u> of <u>red</u> wine.

Students appreciate that the number of stresses can depend on the speed of speaking:

(more slowly)   A <u>bottle</u> of <u>red</u> wine.
(more quickly)   A bottle of <u>red</u> wine.

If asked which they prefer, they usually choose the quicker version. Anticipating that some students will not be able to say it as fast as they would wish, the teacher may offer them an extra stress as support, doctoring the rhythm for their sake, while telling others to say the faster version with the fewer stresses. The choice of stress position may also depend on the sentence rhythm; students can try it out both ways:

<u>How</u> much is that <u>black</u> <u>umbrella</u>?
or   <u>How</u> <u>much</u> is that <u>black</u> <u>umbrella</u>?

Students also realise that the speaker may stress this word or that, without altering the meaning but for the sake of variety, rhythm or even tact as in the following (also from *Streamline Departures*):

Traveller: I've got some whiskey and I've got some
                     cigarettes.
Customs officer: <u>How</u> much whiskey have you got?
          or   How <u>much</u> whiskey have you got?
          or   How much <u>whiskey</u> have you got?

It is particularly constructive when students, having bet on different stresses, defend their choices. Listening and predicting tasks are both highly suitable as homework if the student has access to a cassette player.

Stress for contrasts and comparisons

Another good introduction to sentence stress is the answer where the speaker shifts the stress to different words to highlight the alternating importance. Here is a specially construed exercise, also intended to revise adjectives and nouns:

Teacher: What's a Fiat?   Student: A <u>car</u>.
         And a Citroen?   A <u>French</u> car.
         And a Honda?   A <u>Japanese</u> car.
         And a Fiat?   An <u>Italian</u> car.
         And a Martini?   An <u>Italian</u> <u>drink</u>.
         And a Dubonnet?   A <u>French</u> <u>drink</u>.
         And a Citroen?   A <u>French</u> <u>car</u>.

In case of difficulties, apply the contradiction principle: 'Is a Fiat a

French car?', 'Is a Dubonnet a French car?' When asked, even beginners can say why it is a 'French car' here but 'French car' there, referring to 'repetition' or 'it's not important now'. With a large class it feels like moving stress by remote control.

After this sort of interrogation, the students' sentence stress does improve. This can be turned into a game, too, such as the following.

Good morning, Dr Fisher

Students divide into groups of four to six. One student in each group is Mr Fisher and is issued with his visiting card:

> Mr T Fisher
> 13 Green Street
> London SW7

The other students are each given a question to ask Fisher, as if interviewing him:

A:	Good morning, Dr Fisher.
Fisher:	Mr Fisher.
B:	Are you S. Fisher?
Fisher:	T. Fisher.
C:	You live at 15 Green Street?
Fisher:	No, 13 Green Street.
D:	And that's in SW10?
Fisher:	No, SW7!
E:	I see. Thank you, Dr Fisher.
Fisher:	Mr Fisher.

It is probably best if the teacher takes Mr Fisher's part for the first time. After each round, another student becomes Fisher and the others pass their questions round, so that each has a go at each role.

Questions returned, passed on or repeated

There is another use of stress of prime communicative value, waiting to be learnt: stress in personal questions returned or repeated to someone else. Conversations with students are often one-sided: the teacher asks the questions and the students only answer. A classical case is when at the start of the class, the teacher asks the students all sorts of personal questions: 'What did you do last night?' The students answer, but alas rarely return the question, which in normal life might indicate that they are not interested or feel it impertinent to ask. To spark off a reaction, I sometimes ask 'End of conversation?' Then I say 'Ask me too', hoping someone will say 'What did you do (last night)?' At best they'll return a meagre 'And you?'

The simplest remedy is to write the exchange on the board and ask them where the stress should be the second time, and why. After consideration, they usually agree that *you* is the most important or interesting or new point the second time, the rest being just repetition. Then they do the exchange again, with the teacher or amongst themselves in pairs. However simple the idea, it takes some time to establish the habit. Luckily, stress practice combines well with general language practice especially tenses and *your/yours* and makes good further practice, and revision:

 A (to B): Have you <u>seen</u> my <u>bag</u>?
 B: No.
 A (to C): Have <u>you</u> seen my bag?
 C: No.

Another easy start is when A says something about himself/herself and then asks the same, turning to the next student, who answers and then passes the question on to the next student, chainwise:

 A: My birthday's in <u>July</u>. When's <u>your</u> birthday?
 B: In <u>May</u>. (to C) When's <u>your</u> birthday?
 C: In <u>January</u>. (to D) And when's <u>your</u> birthday?

Note the natural short answer, which also speeds up the practice. You can wind this practice round any number of topics:

 My name's Michael. What's your name?
 I live in the centre. Where do you live?
 I usually get up at seven. When do you get up?

This way, a language drill almost turns into a conversation, with the one constraint that it must be the same question, about the person. 'What's the time?' cannot be used, as you could pass the question round a dozen times without any change of stress.

 More expert students enjoy the challenge of changing the question, thus switching between two stress positions. Students are asked to think of three subjects (such as ecology, modern art, folk music) and write them down. Then they choose one and start asking round:

 A (to B): Are you <u>interested</u> in <u>ecology</u>?
 A (to C): Are <u>you</u> interested in ecology?

After asking three people, they bring up their second item:

 A (to B): Are you interested in <u>modern art</u>?
 A (to C): Are <u>you</u> interested in modern art?

It is best to focus only on the stress in the question here, without going into the stress of the answer as well, as it may have a different stress purpose.

 If encouraged from the beginning, it does not take long for students to use stress in the right way spontaneously. The trick of keeping the conversation going by sending back the question with the stress on *you*, also furthering the students' contact with English-speaking people, is a good enough reason. But it is also a means of practising real language, as in the following situation, where the stress remains on *you*, even when the wording changes:

A (inviting four friends for drinks):

> What would you like, Liz?
> And what are you having, Bill?
> Alan, what do you feel like?
> And you, Mary, what do you fancy?

When students act this out, they sound very fluent despite being at perhaps only early intermediate level.

Stress as an alternative to 'So do I'

There is a good example of interaction between words, stress and meaning. The speaker puts the main stress on the grammatical subject of the sentence, expressing the same meaning as 'So ... I'. For example, the teacher starts by making statements which everyone is likely to agree with:

> T: I like holidays.
> S: I like holidays.
> T: I like holidays in the sun.
> S: I like holidays in the sun.

Asked what 'I like holidays' means, students realise it has to do with 'also', 'too' and 'so do I'. Any number of verbs can be revised via this stress exercise, and it can be done in groups, pairs or all together:

> A: I can drive.   B: I can drive.
>   I've never been to New York.   I've never been to New York.
>
>   I wish I'd bought one.   I wish I'd bought one.

Next, a conversation is set up, where everyone is supposed to agree, but expressing it differently each time:

> A: I'd like to go to India.
> B: I'd like to go to India.
> C: I'd like to go to India, too.
> D: I'd also like to go to India.
> E: So would I.
> F: Me too.

Similarly, 'I don't' can alternate with 'Nor do I'. This is a chance for students to be expressive without complex grammar.

Tests

Because sentence stress, being a logical feature of language, can often be marked on a right/wrong basis, it lends itself well to written tests

and assessments. Students can easily measure their progress periodi-
cally by marking the stress in dialogues listened to or read, with a key
at the back, or in self-contained sentences:

> Underline the words which are contrasted
> and likely to have the main stresses.

> *I live in South London, not North London.*
> *These shoes are a bit small. Have you got a larger pair?*
> *I've got a big brother and she's got a small brother.*
> *You've got green eyes and I've got blue eyes.*
> *I'm an engineer and he's an engineer.*

If schools and examination boards started to include simple tests like
these, the sentence stress skill would soon begin to flourish.

Teachers' problems

Teachers sometimes feel they need a certain amount of background
theory to be able to work on sentence stress with their students.
Unfortunately, there is rarely the time for this sort of study and
students cannot be kept waiting. I have tried to talk about sentence
stress here in the way I often explain it to students, hoping this might
do as initial information for teachers new to the subject. It is possible
that rather less theory is needed and that teachers, like students, can
resort to logic. After all, the aim is not to understand the entire system
but only to encourage our students to take advantage of stress.

It does happen, of course, that teachers too forget the reality and
hammer in the stresses in unnecessary places. But by saying the
sentence spontaneously, imagining a real situation, they should have
no problem finding the natural places for stress in that context. It is
also important that teachers put quotes round the practice sentence on
the board, to remind themselves that it is part of a conversation.

Anyone with difficulties soon resolves them by rehearsing the practice sentence aloud a few times, avoiding being side-tracked by
irrelevant secondary stress. Teachers sometimes express concern that
students will end up overstressing when speaking. In class, you may
need to exaggerate slightly, adding more feeling and energy to the
sentence than native speakers normally do. But if the students, having
got the stress, are encouraged to relax and say the sentence again more
naturally, there is no danger they will go away sounding particularly
stilted.

If done simply, as described, there is no reason why sentence stress
should not be presented as part of the sentence in the beginner's first
week. But just as we teach one use of a tense or one meaning of a
preposition at a time, so it is best to deal with sentence stress step by
step. For example, in the first week we focus on the general stresses:
'Where do you live?' In the next week we introduce a more specific use:

'Where do you live?' The temptation is to go on to: 'Where do you live? or 'Where do you live?'

However, these usages are not of great use to learners, and they do distract the learners from the (to them) really useful usages. Selection and grading has to rule in pronunciation as in grammar and lexis.

The bonus of sentence stress

Short questions

Trying out some sentence stress practice once with young learners in a chain practice ('Do you like Chaplin?, 'Do you like Chaplin?'), I sim-plified the subsequent questions to just 'Do you?' The 10-year-olds took to this like ducks to water. Ever since, I have constantly brought in short questions, partly for stress purposes but also as a natural and economical piece of language, delighting even advanced students. Short questions have enabled me to ban all short answers, such as the following, from my classroom practice:

A: Did you come here by bus?
B: No, I didn't.

The groping for the right auxiliary acts as a lead weight on the conversation and must have cut short many an exchange between foreign and native speakers. Instead, the use of the short question exercises the auxiliaries just as much, and it extends the conversation:

A: Did you come here by bus?
B: No. Did you?

Combined stress and structure practice

As already suggested, a number of structures seem made for joint stress practice. The most evident examples are all the verb constructions, such as the tenses, where the situation can move stress on and off the auxiliary and help to clarify both the form and the concept:

I've opened it.	I have opened it.
I've got a ticket.	I've got a ticket.
I'd have run.	I would have run.
It's being repaired.	It's being repaired.

Any structure with words that can be contrasted can be suitably exercised, such as adjective + noun, comparative adjectives, preposi-tions, word order, adverbs of frequency, as well as the time, dates, money and measures.

The practical sequence for teaching

Many teaching programmes begin by examining the vowel and consonant sounds, then going on to contractions and weak forms, and then, time permitting, to stress and rhythm. To me, this seems back-to-front, since it is the sentence stress that determines which words are unstressed and the speaking speed that dictates just how they are contracted, the vowel and consonant sounds changing accordingly. How is the foreign learner to know which the unstressed words are, without establishing the stresses first?

Psychologically, it also makes sense to start with sentence stress, as students have far less difficulty with it than they have with the sounds. No tears are shed over the correction of stress. Unlike the sounds, it is something they can try out at once in a conversation. And if they are complimented on their good English, it will be because of their sensitive sentence stress rather than their perfect sounds.

The future of stress

The more helpful the language information we can give to learners, the better. This applies not least to sentence stress. Many idioms and phrases come with built-in stress:

> So do I.
> So I do.
> I think so.

There are also numerous words which are habitually stressed, like verbs in the negative (for example, *doesn't, hasn't, couldn't*), and all words with an element of emphasis or the extreme (such as *always, never, only, all, a lot, both, too*).

In a number of cases, certain words are usually unstressed, as in the following phrases:

> Driving a car
> Reading a book
> Writing a letter
> The telephone rang
> The kettle boiled
> The sun shone

A main stress on the verb here could sound daft, so why not tell students about it? It is interesting, too, that adverbial phrases stressed at the beginning of the sentence, are not always stressed at the end:

> Last night, I had a strange dream.
> I had a strange dream last night.

On the <u>wall</u> there was a <u>mirror</u>.
There was a <u>mirror</u> on the wall.

Even if the stress could change, subject to the speaker's thinking, there are undoubtedly numerous cases where the stress is more or less predictable. Foreign learners would find it most useful to see any 'stress-proof' words and phrases marked in coursebooks and dictionaries, so that they knew where they could safely put the stress.

Note

The copyright of this chapter is retained by the author.

Reference

Hartley, B. and Viney, P. (1978) *Streamline Departures* Oxford University Press.

Chapter 7
Interactive Intonation

Joanne Kenworthy
Polytechnic of East London

Introduction

That work on intonation should focus on its role in interaction should be uncontroversial. The major developments in language teaching over the past 15 years, principally the communicative approach, lend support to the notion that learners need practice in using language to communicate. But nonetheless, despite widespread adherence to this approach in other areas of language teaching, there is still a focus in many pronunciation exercises and activities on the individual learner's production and perception. Students work on their own production of modelled contours and use of stress. They are given exercises in which they are presented with recordings or teacher samples of intonation patterns, and they work on accurate processing of these examples by trying to identify pitch movement, stress placement, etc. Such exercises play an important role in 'opening the ears' of learners and helping them to reshape their use of features of pitch and stress towards those of the target language.

But these exercise types also tend to dominate when the goal is practising the active use of intonation and stress placement in conversation. In many exercises designed to do this, the emphasis is still on the production by the individual learners of intonation patterns or stress placement. Such exercises are often opportunities for more realistic use of intonation. However, they still may not reflect what happens in real conversation where meaning is negotiated; where speakers and hearers co-operate; where there are constant joint efforts to understand one another and repair misunderstanding; and where intonation and stress play an important role in the minor diplomacy of everyday human relationships. There is little or no genuine interaction of the type just described in many such activities. As Bachman and Palmer (1984:17) say, 'communication involves two parties and success in communicative performance will always be dependent upon the activities of two people'. In intonation exercises learners should have opportunities to check how well they worked together with the other speaker; how well each responded to the message the other had encoded; and, when one party has obviously misunderstood, how the other party adapted their message. What we need are exercises in which the intonation and stress produced by one speaker are *determined by* and *must be linked to* the intonation and stress used by the other speaker.

Tag questions

To demonstrate these points let us take the example of tag questions. Rising and falling tag questions are one of the most commonly taught uses of intonation. They form part of the intonation syllabus of many coursebooks. In teacher training courses many trainees encounter them as a first example of what intonation is and does, no matter what model of intonation is being taught, and even if no particular model of intonation is being taught. Various explanations of rising and falling tags have been given. In attitudinal approaches, the labels 'uncertainty' and 'certainty' are often applied to rising and falling tags respectively. In functional approaches, falling tags are said to be 'confirming' and rising tags realise the function of 'asking'. In discourse approaches, reference is made to the 'shared knowledge' or expectations of the participants – by using a falling tag the speaker conveys that the proposition of the utterance is one that s/he is assuming is shared with the addressee. This exercise from *On the Move* (Buckley and Prodromou, 1988:72) clearly presents to learners key aspects of the use of tags, and offers opportunities for them to consolidate their awareness and productive skills.

Responding to tag questions

Something crucial is missing from this otherwise sensible exercise, and that is how the addressee responds to a low falling tag question (with reversed polarity). If the addressee does indeed share or accept the proposition in the first part of the utterance, and is therefore going to give the expected confirmation, this confirmation will usually be delivered on a fall in the lower part of the pitch range. There will probably be very little pitch movement and very little duration as well – the fall will be a quick one. Using rising intonation or a fall which begins in the high part of the pitch range will convey a completely different message. In fact, such a response is anomalous and will probably cause confusion and possible communication breakdown. In other words, the responder must make appropriate choices as regards tone and pitch placement.

In discourse models of intonation (e.g. Brazil, 1985) there are three pitch placement options: high, mid, and low. These are realised by the pitch of the onset syllable of a tone group, whether it is higher than, the same as, or lower than the previous tone group. Mid key is used by speakers to show that the information is 'additive'. If a speaker chooses

Section 4·UNIT 14

3 **Listening**

Intonation
a Look at some of the ways we can make questions:

Answer expected

1 Cricket began in the 17th century, didn't it? ...
2 Cricket didn't begin in the 17th century, did it? ...
3 Cricket began in the 17th century, didn't it? ...
4 Cricket didn't begin in the 17th century, did it? ...

Numbers 1 and 3, and 2 and 4 **look** the same but now listen to how they are spoken. Decide on the answer the speaker expects, and fill in the blanks with *Yes*, or *No*, or *?* if the speaker is really asking for information (a genuine 'question').
What makes the difference in meaning between 1 and 3, and between 2 and 4?

b Listen to the following questions and mark the direction of the voice on the 'tag' (which is in italic).

Either: ↗ = A questioning tone
Or: ↘ = The speaker expects agreement

Example (question 1 in **3a** above): ↗
Cricket began in the 17th century, didn't it?

1 Cricket isn't male-dominated, *is it?*
2 Cricket's male-dominated, *isn't it?*
3 Cricket isn't male-dominated, *is it?*
4 Cricket's male-dominated, *isn't it?*

c Listen to some more questions and mark the answer expected (*Yes*, *No* or *?*). Your marks should refer to the questions, not to the text you read in **2a**.

1	2	3	4	5	6	7	8	9	10
□	□	□	□	□	□	□	□	□	□

d Listen again and this time give short answers to the questions by referring to the text in **2a**.

Confirm:
Yes, that's { *true.*
correct.
No, { *right.*

Or
Contradict: *Actually, it is/isn't.*
In fact, it did/didn't.
As a matter of fact, they were/weren't.

(Buckley and Prodromou, 1988:72, by permission of Oxford University Press)

low key, the information in the tone group is somehow 'equivalent' to that in the previous tone group. For example, it may be a repetition or reformulation of a previous tone group. Use of high key signals some kind of contrast with the previous message content.

In discourse intonation, there are two basic choices of tone: fall–rising and falling. Choice of falling tone signals that the information is being treated as 'new' or 'proclaimed' by the speaker. A fall–rise signals that information is being referred to or taken as already negotiated or 'shared' in the interaction between speakers. A simple rising tone is seen as a variant of the fall–rise or referring tone in Brazil's model, and the rise–fall as a variant of the falling or proclaiming tone.

In the rest of this chapter, the following symbols will be used to represent these tones: fall $\searrow$, rise $\nearrow$, fall–rise $\searrow\!\!\nearrow$, and rise–fall $\wedge$. Tone group boundaries are shown by //. The tonic syllable is in capitals and underlined, and stressed syllables are in small capitals. Key is shown by the placement of the text in relation to the line: above the line for 'high', on the line for 'mid', and below the line for 'low'.

Contradicting expectations

With regard to the above speaker intonation choices, consider the difference between the following two tag question exchanges. In the first exchange, speaker B uses a fall in high key; in the second exchange, B uses a low key fall:

A: //$\searrow$CRICKet is male-<u>DOM</u>inated//$\searrow$ //
                                                            ISN'T IT

B: //$\searrow$ YES   it IS //$\searrow$ //$\searrow$ //

A: //$\searrow$CRICKet is male-<u>DOM</u>inated//$\searrow$ //
                                                            ISN'T it

B: //$\searrow$ $\searrow$ //
        YES//   it IS

It is the low key fall in the second exchange that seems most appropriate. When B chooses a high key fall, s/he seems to be saying 'obviously' or 'How could you possibly think otherwise?' Why? Because a fall from high has the effect of identifying a contrast. So the responder (B) doesn't seem to be recognising that A is representing the point as shared knowledge. Add increased volume and it becomes even worse – we have one interlocutor (B) casting aspersions on the judgement and beliefs of the other. In other words, it *could* be heard as a rebuff, as a kind of assault on the speaker for having bothered to state the obvious. This effect is produced mainly by the lack of 'pitch concord'. Speakers often match their contributions in terms of key. A shift upwards in pitch placement by one speaker will often be echoed or matched by the other speaker. This pitch concord in terms of pitch placement or key is used to show 'mutuality' ('we are in sync') and lack of pitch concord is used to signal lack of mutuality.[1]

Conversational openings

The (mis)use of pitch placement in exchanges like the above is particularly 'undiplomatic' – one could even say 'dangerous' – because of the
way falling tag questions are used. In British culture, it is very
important to fill silence, and when having a pleasant chat with another
person (particularly someone not well known), people rarely raise
controversial issues and get the conversation going in this way. Instead
they actively look for propositions that will be agreed with – topics that,
because there is mutual agreement, will help build a sense of solidarity.

This may be one reason why the weather is chosen so often as a topic
for conversational openers in Britain. Both parties are experiencing the
same weather conditions and assessments of what is good or bad
weather vary little between individuals. Therefore, the chances that
you will say 'Another beautiful sunny day, isn't it?' and your interlocutor will disagree with you, are very slight indeed.

Even a conversation which, on the surface, seems like an exchange of
views and opinions is often really an exchange of propositions which
each participant thinks the other will agree with. The participants may
end up not really knowing much about what the others actually think.
But the solidarity which results from a conversation which seems to be
full of agreement can be quite important in the process of 'establishing
friendly relations'.

So, in summary we can say that the exercise in *On the Move* gives the
students practice in recognising the contrast between a rising tag and a
low falling tag, and therefore helps in producing these. However, what
it does not help them to do is to signal to the other speaker that *their*
signal about expectations and shared information has been picked up.
That is, it is not really an interactive use of intonation.

Mitigation

So far we have discussed the use of low falling pitch in response to a low
falling tag when the tag questionee agrees with the proposition, that is,
is answering in the expected way. What happens when someone
addresses a tag question to you and signals through the use of the low
falling tag that they think you believe the proposition to be true or
accurate, but they have got it wrong – you do not believe this? From
what we said above, according to the options open to speakers in a
discourse model of intonation, a response with a fall in high key,
denying the proposition, would seem to be appropriate. However, this is
a 'danger' point in the conversation, because a low fall inhibits a
contradictory response. The response must therefore be carefully
negotiated. The strategy used in many cases by the one who is going to
counter expectations is to 'soften' this by the use of a phrase like
'actually' or 'in fact', or 'well ...' or simply a non-verbal filler. The
exercise in *On the Move* draws learners' attention to these expressions,
but it does not mention the intonation used in these unexpected replies.

The use of intonation which accompanies these responses seems to depend to some extent on the content of the proposition. If A has made a statement which relates to B's biography – some fact or point about which B is the only and ultimate authority – and if it is wrong, then B may not feel the need to mitigate or soften the blow. S/he may use a high falling pitch movement (or proclaiming tone in high key) to clearly show the contrast:

> A: //↘You're John's SISTER//↘   //
> AREN'T you

> NO   I'm an old FRIEND
> B: //↘   //↘   //

But if the statement is not part of B's biography, but a comment about the 'outside world', or if it is a matter of personal opinion, then B will probably use an initial mitigator such as 'actually', 'well' or 'uhh'. S/he may even avoid high key and a falling tone, opting instead for fairly minimal pitch movement. It depends on whether B wants to tackle the difference of views (in discourse terms the 'lack of convergence') head-on or smooth over it, agreeing to some extent in order to establish some solidarity.

> A: //↘It's got a REALLy good ATMosphere//↘↗ this PUB//
>
> //↘DOESN'T it //

> B: //↘↗ WELL //↘I preFER things//↘a bit more
>
> QUIet//↘↗ but this is OK//↘in small DOSES//

Notice the mitigating word 'well', the use of hedges such as 'a bit' and the way B offers some agreement. Contrast this with the following reply:

> B: //↘not to MY MIND//↘do you really LIKE//
> //↘↗ all this JOSTling and NOISE//

Here B tackles the lack of convergence head-on.

From the above discussion it is clear that although tag questions may have become an ubiquitous part of the intonation syllabus because they seem so neat and straightforward, this is not the case at all. This is especially clear when we begin to look at how and why speakers use them in conversation, and how the content of the proposition determines their lexical and intonational choices as well. And then if we take into account cultural norms and personalities – whether people tend to be 'up-front' about their opinions and feelings, even when these are opposed to those held by their interlocutor, or tend to smooth out any lack of convergence – then the picture of tags as a straightforward use of intonation begins to break down. But this is not to be regretted, because it shows how rich a signalling system intonation is and why control of it is so valuable to learners.

Classroom activities

How can we work on these aspects of tag questions? Clearly mechanical perception and production exercises are not good enough, nor are exercises which do not require learners to make choices about how to respond. We must build upon the *On the Move* exercise and others like it, and this may require a bit of ingenuity and even some mendacity or double dealing. Here is a possible activity. It could be used after there had been some perception work on tags and/or some work on production.

1   Ask members of the class to write down between five and 10 simple facts about themselves: where they come from; their family members and what they do; how long they have been in a particular place; where they have lived before or visited on holiday; what their career goals are; etc.
2   Collect these in before the activity and (here is the small bit of double dealing) change one of the facts towards the end of each list. So if it read 'I lived in Switzerland for three years', amend this to, say, 'five years'.
3   In class, divide the students into groups of three and redistribute the slips of paper. The facts about one member in the group are given to another member of that group. That member is to practise using low falling tags as s/he talks to the student about what they have put down in their mini-biography. The third member of the group is supposed to listen and monitor the use of falling tags.
4   Circulate to see that all is going well. If tape recorders are available then the students can record the activity.

All should go smoothly until the tag questioner gets to the fact that the teacher has fiddled with. Various things may happen: the groups may come to the conclusion that some trick is being played or something has been mixed up and look at the facts as written down, or they may think they have got the wrong bits of paper etc. Reconvene the class and discuss how the activity went. The discussion should cover the following points:

(a)   How did students respond to tag questions which contained an accurate proposition? Did they use the right lexis? Did the questioner use falling intonation? Did the responder use a low fall? Ask a group who did well to demonstrate or replay a recording. Alternatively, play a prepared recording of native speakers doing the exercise and using the appropriate pitch movements.
(b)   How did the tag questionee respond when the information was inaccurate and yet the questioner was expecting confirmation? Did they 'let them down easy' intonation-wise or contradict with a high fall?
(c)   Did they use any of the typical mitigators? If not, introduce these into the discussion.

The 'observer' member of the group should be very active in the discussion. The teacher will have had to decide beforehand what terminology to use and whether points such as the fact that B was the ultimate authority on these biographical facts played a part. The activity can be redone to give students a chance to change roles and to consolidate their control and appreciation of tags.

An extra activity could be inserted here if there are two class members with the same native language. They could quickly translate the activity into their native language and class members and teachers could listen for the use of intonation. There may even be particular mitigating lexis involved in that language to compare with English 'well', 'actually', etc.

The main teaching point is that the way you use intonation should be linked to what your conversational partner has done. But with appropriate groups the cultural dimension could be discussed. Is British culture unlike other cultures in the way people agree and disagree? For example, are other cultures more 'up front' about differences in opinions? What do speakers do when someone else's assumptions are false? How far do different cultures regard correcting another speaker as impolite?

An observed breakdown

The discussion so far has indicated how inappropriate intonation signals can impede the smooth flow of conversation. Let us consider an example of this.[2]

N is a learner of English from Spain who lodges with L. Their relationship is cordial, and they tend to have chats about everyday events, usually in the kitchen. L had mentioned to me that talking with N was 'hard work' and I asked her if she would make a tape-recording of one of their chats. Quite typically L decided to get some talk by asking N questions about herself. But she has known N for a few months so many of her questions are of the 'have-I-got-this-right' type. N seems to have expected this, and her short laugh in line 2 seems to say 'I knew she'd start with that one!'

```
1  L:  //↘so how LONG have you been in ENGland//
2  N:  (laugh) //↘↗ I have been LIVE in ENGland//↘six MONTHS//
3  L:  // ↘↗ um HM// ↘↗ and have you been in LONdon//
          ↘↗ the whole TIME//
4  N:  //↘long TIME//
5  L:  //↘have you been in LONdon//↘the whole TIME//
       // ↘↗              //↘weren't you somewhere ELSE//
          in ENGland
       //↘in CHELtenham//
```

6 N: //\YEAH//\before in CHELtenham//\   //
                                    YES
    //\↗ I live in CHELtenham//\for THREE MONTH//
    //\↗ from OcTober//\until DeCEMber//
7 L: //\m HM//\and what were you DOing in CHELtenham//
8 N: //\↗ WELL//\↗ in   CHELtenham   I   STUdy//\in   St
    PAUL and St MAry// \↗ and in DeCEMber//\
                                                I   work   in
    the COFfee shop
9 L: //\and what was it LIKE//\did you enJOY it//
    //\↗   //
        LIVing there
                        eh NO
10 N: //\   //\I NEVer enjoy it//\↗ beFORE in
    CHELtenham//\↗ NO//\it was very . . . a LITtle HARD//
    //\NOW I enJOY it//\   //
                        YEAH
11 L: //\   //
        but you hadn't studied ENGlish in Spain beFORE
            NO
12 N: //\ //\I NEVer studied ENGlish// \↗ in SPAIN
    before//\only three MONTHS//\before I CAME to
    ENGland//
13 L: //\   //\↗ so just THREE months in SPAIN//\
        YEAH   and SIX
                        //
    months in ENGland
14 N: //\   //\   //
        YEAH   THAT right

At the beginning all seems to be going smoothly, except for N's misunderstanding of 'the whole time'. N uses falling tones to mark new information ('six months', 'from October to December', 'I work in the coffee shop', etc.). She uses referring tones for shared information ('in Cheltenham', 'in England', etc.). There is also pitch concord between the two. This occurs at lines 5 and 6 (mid–mid) and lines 7 and 8 (mid–mid).

But at line 9 L asks a question in mid key, and N shifts to high key in her response to show the contrast of her experience with L's choice of the verb 'enjoy'. L then uses low key and referring tone on 'but you hadn't studied English in Spain before'. Her choice of these is probably designed to signal that 'having not studied much English' was the reason for N not enjoying herself in Cheltenham – the two are 'equative'. N responds with a high key fall. She clearly has not heard L's negative formulation (she thinks L has said 'but you studied English . . .'). She also has not interpreted L's use of low key as signalling the relationship between 'not knowing much English' and finding things 'hard'. Because she has misread or missed all these signals, she thinks she has to deny L's incorrect statement ('you studied English in Spain') and she does so with a fall in high key.

L is clearly not expecting a high key response to her low key statement; what she probably expected was something similar to N's response at line 6 ('yeah'). Note all the 'work' she does in line 13 to repair this minor breakdown. Lexically, her initial 'yeah' signals agreement or convergence; then she chooses to repeat the whole point introducing this with 'so', which serves as a signal to say 'I am establishing our shared knowledge'; she then tries to establish more common ground by echoing N's 'only three months' with 'just three months'; finally, she uses low key twice to mark points as shared. N does seem to take all this in and agrees in low key – 'yeah that right'.

This minor 'blip' in the smooth unfolding of talk is interesting in two respects: (*i*) it shows us how important a 'state of convergence' is to participants in a conversation – if they do so much work to establish it and repair it then it certainly must be important, and (*ii*) it gives us a clear pointer towards a very specific teaching point, namely the use of low key statements, usually with a negative formulation, which the speaker uses to show that two aspects of the message content are connected or 'equative' (here the connection is cause-result) and which they expect the other to confirm. Learners need to be trained in hearing these low key statements. They seem to be just as frequently used as falling tag questions, perhaps even more frequently. If learners consistently misunderstand them, then native/non-native conversations will not unfold as smoothly as they might.

Agreeing and disagreeing

In discussing such aspects of conversational interaction as the use of tag questions and of negative formulations such as L's, it becomes apparent that these are part of a more general category or function, and that is the area of agreeing and disagreeing. We need to explore how speakers make intonation choices when their goal is to either agree or to disagree with a previous speaker. In a comparative study carried out by Koester (1990) on German and English some interesting patterns emerged.

Koester used two tasks: (*i*) speakers were presented with a selection of numbers and had to discuss how they would say the numbers and what they would represent, e.g. 748, 021-3370452; (*ii*) they had to talk about various hairstyles shown in photographs and discuss whether they liked them or not.[3] Three informant groups were used: (*a*) native English speakers speaking standard southern British English; (*b*) native German speakers speaking standard High German, and (*c*) intermediate German learners of English speaking in English. The informants were tape-recorded as they did the tasks in pairs. Koester used Brazil's model of discourse intonation as a basis for analysis.

In the data most agreeing occurred in mid key. Since mid key is chosen to present information as 'additive' it would seem to be the norm for agreeing – you 'add' the information that you agree with a particular proposition made by a previous speaker. When speakers chose low key, it seemed that the speaker was agreeing in a way that was much like a repetition, or projecting their agreement as somehow already negotiated. For example, in discussing one hairstyle which both participants clearly did not like, the interaction ended as follows (Koester, 1990:85; German speakers speaking German, translated):

A: //↘very unflattering//
B: //↘   //↘   //
    yes   that's true

Note that A could easily have decided to use a low falling tag ('very unflattering, isn't it?') and B would most likely have responded in low key.

Koester also found that high key seemed to be used when the agreement was particularly enthusiastic. He accounts for this in the following way:

> Using high keys means that the element chosen is contrasted to anything else that could have occurred in that slot. Thus by agreeing with someone in high key speakers commit themselves to the other person's opinion as opposed to any other. To use a paraphrase: mid key would seem to imply simply 'I agree with this'; whereas high key implies an additional element, 'I agree with this *and nothing else*'. (Koester, 1990:86–87)

In one example B agrees with A about '3.14' representing a date and then adds a comment in mid key (native English speakers; only relevant utterances are transcribed for intonation):

A: Time, three fourteen
B: mhm
A: //↘and DATE//↘the FOURteenth of   //
                                 MARCH
B: //↘oh YEAH//↘that's the aMERican way//↘BACKwards//
                                       (Koester, 1990:90)

In terms of tone choice, both choices were made by speakers, but the fall–rise seemed to be used for a more 'matter of fact' agreement, and the fall for a more affirmative one. The affirmative effect which can be attached to the falling tone seems to come from the informing function of this tone.

For the function of disagreeing, Koester's data show a predominance of falling tone in mid or high key. Speakers seem to 'overtly inform each other of their disagreement' (Koester, 1990:91). In using high key with its meaning of contrast, the disagreement comes across as stronger. It implies 'I think this and not what you think'. But interestingly, in initiating disagreement, speakers may use the fall–rise tone to avoid being too assertive about disagreement. This has echoes of attitudinal approaches to intonation, where the fall–rise is said to be used to show 'reluctant dissent' (Koester, 1990:95). (Native English speakers)

1   A: //↘THIS is one of my FAvourite hairstyles//

2   B: //∨↗   YES i —   //

3   A: //∨↗ except that THAT blond HAIR//↘doesn't SUIT her white FACE//

4   B: No and I always think they're a bit masculine, those hairstyles on girls. (Koester, 1990:92)

A further signal that there is lack of convergence here is the breaking of pitch concord. A's utterance at 1 is in mid key; in responding B chooses high key. From what B goes on to say in line 4, it is clear that B's 'yes' in line 2 is a token agreement. This can be compared to the use of key in the conversation between L and N. Pitch concord or the breaking of it are important signals of the state of convergence between speakers.

Disagreement sequences seemed generally to be longer than agreement sequences. Especially when the conversation revolves around personal opinions (as the hairstyle task does), speakers downgrade their disagreement – they try to make it less 'confrontational'. They use token agreement (the typical British 'yes, but . . .'), insert requests for clarification, and use hedges such as 'sort of', 'a bit', to soften their disagreement.

Classroom activities

The two tasks Koester used, and others like them, clearly offer a lot of opportunities for work on intonation. Similar procedures to those suggested for tag questions could be used in the classroom. The teacher asks the learners to do the tasks and then focuses on how they used intonation. Learners could then be encouraged to explore the speaker choices in various ways. For instance, after having done the tasks and analysed their performance, a particular student could be assigned the role of 'confrontational disagree-er' and have to use falling tones and high key to constantly break pitch concord. Another could be given the role of the 'ultra-diplomat' who tries to agree as much as possible with what others say. Again, in exploring intonation, learners will be made aware of the complexity of conversation and of the cultural differences and conventions.

Establishing common knowledge

As the discussion so far has illustrated, the mutual knowledge, shared beliefs and assumptions of the participants are of central concern in the joint activity of communicating. It follows that if speakers fail to recognise and acknowledge the status of information, some element of co-operativeness will be missing from the conversation. The participant who thinks that his or her contribution has not been 'acknowledged' may feel the need to carry out repairs. S/he may use utterances such as 'Yes, I just said that', 'I just said so', 'That's what I said/meant' or 'You don't need to tell me that' in order to 'stake a claim' on information.

Conversational interactions are only mere exchanges of facts in certain contexts and, even when one party is clearly in the role of information provider, there is a great deal of talk which confirms and makes explicit the information that has been given. Speakers also spend a great deal of talk in finding out exactly what information is shared and what is not. In a recent article, Scotton and Bernstein (1988) compared the dialogues in coursebooks about asking for and receiving directions with real examples of how people give directions. These had been collected on a university campus. One clear difference was the way in which direction-givers established how much the asker knew about the environs. Checking utterances like 'Do you know the . . .' or 'Have you been here before?' were very frequent. They found that coursebook models of direction-giving were distinctly lacking in this area of establishing common knowledge. They did not, therefore, prepare learners for the type of language typical of such transactions. Speakers are constantly at risk of assuming too much knowledge or too little knowledge on the part of their interlocutor. Any message we send must be suited to what the listener already knows or does not know. The joint establishment of common ground is crucial in conversation.

A classroom activity

Sending signals about the status of information is such a pervasive concern of speakers that it should not be necessary to design special activities to introduce, practise and consolidate this speech skill. All teachers need is coursebooks with activities which stimulate genuine exchanges. Then it is a matter of exploiting these activities in coursebooks, of spotting the opportunities.

The following activity was designed for grammar practice by Ur (1988). It was designed to practise the simple present tense forms. It is such an engaging and universally interesting activity that it would suit any level. The teacher plays the class the theme music of a film. There are even collections of famous film music available which can be used for this. Alternatively, the teacher can play the opening title sequence from a video of a film. Learners listen and then, in pairs or groups, try to decide what kind of film it is – a thriller, a romance, etc; a modern or old film; what country it was made in; and so on.

This activity would typically stimulate conversations such as the following:[4]

T: at the beginning the music is oriental . . . do you say oriental? – and then we hear the Marseillaise.
E: it sounds like an old film . . . maybe about World War Two.

P: yes I think it's a war film.
M: me also . . . a war film.

These speakers have used various syntactic and lexical signals of common ground: 'yes', 'me also', and the repetition of 'World War Two'/'a war film'. But if the appropriate intonation and stress placement were not used to reflect the status of the information and the agreement, then the interaction would be flawed. For example, if P does not use referring tone and/or low key on 'I think it's a war film', then he does not seem to be acknowledging or being responsive to E's contribution. P may give the impression of being so obsessed with putting his own idea across that he is ignoring the convergence of ideas and, in not conveying these, has lost an opportunity to build solidarity.

Of course this may be the case – people do get so involved with their own reactions and feelings that they ignore what others are saying, and expressing convergence takes second place to the expression of their own feelings and opinions. In a conversation you may realise that someone has just said something that you were about to say, but you are so wound up in your own response and perceptions that you feel you must say it too. To your mind it feels like your 'property'. That this happens in the real world does not invalidate 'expressing convergence' as part of the intonation syllabus. The motivation for including it in our intonation syllabus is to make sure that learners are aware of how English speakers signal shared meanings (perceptive skills) and to make sure that they are realising their intentions (productive control).

What if for another participant the music conjured up a different scenario? This would be signalled by high key falls in order to show 'contrast':

                                                           GAND

  B: // \\↗ //WELL \\I thought it was a propa   a film//

Note again the use of 'well' as a mitigator. B might also break pitch concord on 'well' to show lack of convergence.

This exercise, although originally designed for grammar practice, has great potential for practising and/or consolidating the use of intonation in information management – signalling common ground or signalling a contrast. How can one organise the activity to draw attention to this aspect? There are a wide range of possibilities.

As a grammar practice activity the teacher would probably have done a presentation or revision of the present tense forms and as the students were doing the activity they would be aware that they were practising these forms. Present tense forms would be the only focus for teacher correction. In order to focus on intonation, the teacher could ask one or two groups to tape-record their joint discussions. These could then be replayed and the use of high falls versus low key fall–rises could be explored and/or checked. Students who had been equipped with some way of transcribing falls and rises could make a partial transcript of what they had said to each other and then mark stress placement and pitch movement. Even if all is well, time has not been ill-spent;

learners will gain confidence in their use of the language and increase their own awareness of the complexity of the signals they are capable of sending.

The teacher could also choose a report-back format. Students discuss in small groups or pairs and reach a consensus or tabulate their reactions. Then there is the report-back in which each group tells the whole class how they reacted. This must be done group by group, and the second group's report should be *responsive* to the first group's, the third to both the first and second, and so on. Again, even with native speakers this may not happen because individuals are often bound up in their own reactions. If this does happen then the teacher can take on the role of summariser and thus present an appropriate model for the learners. Alternatively, one student could be nominated to take minutes, write a short report and then read it aloud. In order to do this, s/he must visit each group. Groups could also write their own mini-reports on OHP transparencies. The separate reports could be reworked into one consecutive report which makes clear the convergences and divergences of reactions. When this is read aloud, the intonation must reflect these. This procedure will give lots of opportunities for working on given/new distinctions at the level of lexis and syntax, as well as intonation. There is no reason why an activity which starts out with a grammar focus cannot become an intonation activity and then return to a focus on syntax or lexis – this is true integration of all the language skills.

If students are having difficulty showing contrast and convergence through pitch direction and key placement, then a simpler version of the activity can be used. This has a multiple choice format. Students have a response sheet with about four choices for each piece of theme music. As they listen to each piece in turn they tick one box. Then the results are collated by the teacher going around the class. This produces simple exchanges like the following:

A: I put thriller
B: I put Western
C: romance
D: thriller
E: thriller

The intonation should fit the convergence or contrast of response. If, for example, D says 'thriller' with the same high or mid falling contour as A, then this does not recognise their sameness. It is not wrong; it is inappropriate. Note if two identical responses are very far apart, say six turns, then a fall could be used. Speakers have a choice about when to show convergence and when not to.

This simple idea has yet more potential. The students will probably want to know the 'answer' – 'Was that music what I thought it was or was I way off the mark?' Some students may even recognise the music and be eager to tell the others. If their opinion about a point is confirmed, speakers often express their moment of glory as follows:

//↘I THOUGHT // ↘↗ it was a THRILLer//

The use of intonation clearly reflects the convergence between the real world and the speaker's opinion. Some of the pitch movement will be on 'thought' and the confirmed piece of information will have a fall–rise. On the other hand, if they are not in accord with the facts they may respond thus:

//↘↗ oh I THOUGHT//↘it was a $\overline{\text{WES}}$ tern//

putting a high fall on the point of information that is in contrast to the real state of the world.

In order to focus specifically on these patterns, the teacher could simply put the sentence pattern on the board, reveal the true answer for each piece of music and then ask learners to produce the response appropriate to them.

Once the importance of this responsive use of intonation to signal common ground has been established and worked on, then it should not be neglected. It must be continually consolidated, especially if some students are having difficulty with, say, the fall–rises. Many course-books present ideal opportunities to do this in the form of activities which involve students in registering their preferences, likes, dislikes or opinions on a form and comparing their responses with those of other students. If the tape-recordings accompanying the coursebook have recordings of native speakers doing these activities, then this is an ideal resource for perceiving and practising intonation patterns. If they do not, then a group of native speakers can be asked to record one of the tasks.

Conclusion

Intonation is not the 'icing on the cake', but a basic ingredient of the mix. Because of this, any exercise which promotes interaction should also provide opportunities to practise and consolidate 'interactive intonation'. Intonation comes alive for learners (and teachers) when they realise how important it is in everyday communication.

Notes

1   In a recent masterclass on American accents for British actors, Joan Washington, an accent coach, drew attention to the constant use of pitch concord in American English conversation. She termed this 'picking up on the other's pitch' and described it as a characteristic feature of American intonation.

2   I am grateful to Louise Elkins of Longman for supplying me with this recording.

3 Both tasks were from Willis and Willis (1988).
4 This conversation was produced by a group of advanced German learners of English.

References

Bachman, L. and Palmer, A. (1984) 'Some Comments on the Terminology of Language Testing' *Communicative Competence Approaches to Language Proficiency Assessment* C. Riveria (ed.) Multilingual Matters, Clevedon.

Brazil, D. (1985) *The Communicative Value of Intonation* Monograph No. 8 University of Birmingham: English Language Research.

Buckley, P. and Prodromou, L. (1988) *On the Move* Oxford University Press.

Koester, A. (1990) 'Intonation in Agreeing and Disagreeing in English and German' in Hewings, M. (ed.) *Papers in Discourse Intonation* Monograph No. 16 University of Birmingham: English Language Research.

Scotton, C. and Bernstein, J. (1988) 'Natural Conversation as a Model for Textbook Dialogue' *Applied Linguistics* 9:4.

Ur, P. (1988) *Grammar Practice Activities* Cambridge University Press.

Willis, J. and Willis, D. (1988) *Collins COBUILD English Course Book 1* Collins, London.

Chapter 8
Phonetic Symbols in the Dictionary and in the Classroom

Paul Tench
Centre for Applied English Language Studies, University of Wales, Cardiff

Introduction

For a very long time – indeed centuries – teachers, linguists and scientists have used a set of special symbols to represent the sounds of a language. The symbols were not in fact invented by the great Professor Henry Sweet (1845–1912) but were in existence, and in use, long before his time. Ellis and Bell used phonetic symbols earlier in the nineteenth century in their studies in dialectology and communications, respectively. However, it was mainly Henry Sweet who was responsible for introducing them into language teaching.

The language teaching profession was undergoing a momentous revolution in the final quarter of the nineteenth century, with the emergence of new methodologies and approaches which broke the mould of the traditional 'grammar-translation' method. The new ideas included the promotion of the spoken form of languages and an ability to pronounce them accurately, to balance (or even overturn) the attention that had traditionally been given to the written form, reading, writing and grammar. Sweet was in the vanguard of this new movement and, as the leading linguist and phonetician of his time, his influence was felt throughout the language teaching profession, not only in Britain, but in Europe, too.

Sweet promoted the use of phonetic symbols as an aid in teaching foreign languages (see Henderson, 1971). He drew attention to the need to distinguish between *details* of sounds in what he called a 'narrow' transcription, and *primary sounds* in 'broad' transcription. He is thus credited with the earliest expression of the phoneme principle in Britain, and was one of its earliest proponents in Europe.

It is not surprising that an Englishman should realise the potential of phonetic symbols in language teaching and in the description of the pronunciation system of a language. We need no reminder of the huge discrepancy that exists between English pronunciation and its representation in traditional orthography. Discrepancies, on a lesser scale, also exist in other European languages, and so it was not surprising that European scholars supported each other in the formation of the International Phonetic Association (IPA) in 1886.

The pioneering work of Sweet was disseminated at the turn of the century by the industry and enthusiasm of H.E. Palmer in the English language teaching world, and by Daniel Jones and Ida Ward at the University of London. Through them, use of phonetic symbols became more widespread, and the symbols themselves became a symbol of the new determination to incorporate pronunciation and the spoken form of language as essential ingredients in language teaching. However, there was a divergence of opinion between Jones and Ward as to the symbols they chose to represent the vowels of English, and this divergence has bedevilled the ELT profession ever since.

Why are there different sets of symbols?

The Received Pronunciation of English has a set of 20 vowels, including the diphthongs, but excluding /ɔə/, which is gradually disappearing and for many has merged with /ɔː/, e.g. *core* with *caw*. Thus there are eight diphthongs and 12 (relatively) 'pure' or simple vowels. Of these 12, five are distinguished from the other seven by requiring approximately twice the length of time for pronunciation – the so-called 'long vowels', as found in such words as *bead, pool, harm, court* and *word*. Five of the seven 'short vowels' are reasonably closely associated phonetically with the five long vowels, and it is the linguistic relationship between these five short vowels and the long vowels that lay at the heart of the Jones–Ward divergence. The five short vowels in question are found in such words as *bid, pull, ham, cot* and *(for)ward*.

However, there is not only a distinction of length in the 10 vowels concerned, but also distinctions in the exact positioning of the tongue; so, although it is possible to associate the vowels of, for instance, *bead* and *bid, pool* and *pull* in certain general terms (for example, front close vowels; back close vowels), there are, in fact, the two distinguishing factors: length of articulation and positioning of the tongue. Linguistic phoneticians realised, nevertheless, that it was actually redundant to draw attention to *both* features, as one feature would always also presuppose the other. Ward chose to highlight the difference in tongue position, by using separate symbols for each of the vowels and by omitting any indication of length. Jones, on the other hand, chose to highlight the difference in length, by using the colon as a phonetic symbol (ː) and by reducing the number of other symbols; thus /i/ represented a short vowel (without the /ː/) as in *bid*, and /iː/ represented a long vowel as in *bead*. Notice then the very troublesome ambiguity of the /i/ symbol; Ward used /ɪ/ for the short vowel of *bid* and /i/ for the long vowel of *bead*. Thus /bid/ was *bead* for Ward and *bid* for Jones!

The two systems can be set side by side for comparison:

Ward		Jones
i	*bead*	iː
ɪ	*bid*	i
ɛ	*bed*	e
æ	*bad*	æ
ɑ	*bard*	ɑː
ɒ	*cod*	ɔ
ɔ	*cord*	ɔː
ʊ	*pull*	u
u	*pool*	uː
ʌ	*bud*	ʌ
ɜ	*bird*	əː
ə	*(cup)board*	ə

The two systems extend to the diphthongs:

Ward		Jones
eɪ	*hay*	ei
oʊ	*hoe*	ou
aɪ	*high*	ai
aʊ	*how*	au
ɔɪ	*boy*	ɔi
ɪə	*beer*	iə
ɛə	*bear*	eə
ʊə	*poor*	uə

Although Ward's system was more accurate phonetically, it was Jones's system that became more popular – because it was simpler, both in respect to the *number* of actual symbols required (10 as opposed to Ward's 15) and the *familiarity* of the symbols (most of the 10 were from the 'English' alphabet and punctuation). They were simpler to learn, simpler to use and simpler to write, type and print.

Jones's system was further popularised in the successive editions of the Everyman's *English Pronouncing Dictionary*, which he first published in 1917. His system prevailed for the 60 years of its 13 editions, until it was completely revised by Gimson. Through Jones's scholarly works and the dictionary, his system of symbols became standard throughout the world for representing the Received Pronunciation of English.

The system was not without its difficulties, however, in the classroom. Many pronunciation exercise books followed the pattern of illustrating the vowel system of English by allocating a page to each vowel, with plenty of examples in orthography and in broad phonetic transcription, and then a page to contrast between associated vowels, with plenty of examples of 'minimal pairs'. However, most teachers of English in the world are not native speakers; they would see /iː/ printed prominently on one page, and /i/ on the next, and they were taught that the difference between the vowels was mainly a matter of length. However, such a difference rarely featured in their mother tongue, and although many of these teachers attempted to maintain some distinction, most were more impressed with the identity of the symbols than with the difference of length, and thus the opposition of *bead* and *bid*, *leave* and *live*, *sleep* and *slip*, etc. was lost. If the /ɪ/ symbol had been prominently displayed for the *bid* vowel, then teachers would have been more aware of the differences between the vowels. This was my experience in Nigeria and others have agreed not only from other parts of Africa, but from the rest of the world, too.

Furthermore, experiments have shown that native speakers of English rely more on the auditory effect of differences in tongue position than they do on the auditory effect of length, for the perception of the various vowels of English. This native speaker reaction was taken into account by Gimson when he proposed his own solution to the problem in 1962. His solution is quoted at length from the fourth edition of his *Introduction to the Pronunciation of English*:

> The solution used in the following pages is one which does not seek ultimate economy of categories, gives a good deal of explicit information in the notation about the phonetic realization of the phonemes (especially the relation of quality and quantity), and takes some account of the RP speaker's own feelings as to the distinctive vowel counters which he uses. We will, therefore, treat 20 vocalic phonemes, made up of the following vowels or vowel glides:
>
> 7 *short:* /ɪ, e, æ, ɒ, ʊ, ʌ, ə/
> 5 *long* (relatively pure): /iː, uː, ɑː, ɔː, ɜː/
> 3 *long* (glides to [ɪ]): /eɪ, aɪ, ɔɪ/
> 2 *long* (glides to [ʊ]): /əʊ, aʊ/
> 3 *long* (glides to [ə]): /ɪə, ɛə, ʊə/   Gimson (1989:99)

The advantage of Gimson's system is that it is more explicit than either Jones's or Ward's, and this is a help to English language teachers. The distinction between /iː/ and /ɪ/, and most of the other pairs of long and short vowels in English, is critical, and the dual marking of both length and tongue position is useful. (I now wish I had marked length in the transcription used in my *Pronunciation Skills*, Tench, 1981.)

Gimson's system gradually replaced Jones's as the standard set of symbols for English RP. Gimson himself converted the Everyman's *English Pronouncing Dictionary* in its fourteenth edition (1977) to his system. Successive editions of his *Introduction* each decade (1970, 1980, 1989) established it as the standard British work on English pronunciation, and a number of new editions of pronunciation exercise books and manuals switched to his system. For example, compare the first (1967) and second (1980) editions of O'Connor's *Better English Pronunciation*, Trim's *English Pronunciation Illustrated* (1960 and 1980), and the *Oxford Advanced Learner's Dictionary of Current English*. Most British publications in ELT now conform to Gimson's system. When Wells

launched the new *Longman Pronunciation Dictionary* (1990), he public-
ly announced that he deliberately resisted the temptation of altering
the system of symbols, in order to ensure a degree of stability – a policy
which will be welcomed by thousands (if not millions) around the world.

However, differences are still likely to emerge, for three reasons. The
first is change in pronunciation. We have already noted the demise of
the /ɔə/ diphthong. Also, Gimson introduced the /əʊ/ symbol for the *go*
diphthong in recognition of the change that had taken place 'in recent
years' in the position of the tongue at the start of the diphthongal glide;
see Gimson (1989:134–6). This has, however, been contested by Wynn
as being too extreme (Wynn, 1987:xiii) and thus, in this respect, there is
a transcriptional difference between two systems, in the matter of
change: Gimson has /gəʊ/; Wynn has /goʊ/. Another change, which
Wells has promoted, is the 'half-way' vowel between /iː/ and /ɪ/ which
occurs regularly in unstressed final position in words like *happy*.
Traditional RP has /ɪ/; most other accents have /iː/. Increasingly, RP
speakers are heard using /iː/ or at least a short version of that vowel in
such words, and in words where the opposition between /iː/ and /ɪ/ is
'neutralised', e.g. *obviate* (see Wells, 1990:xviii). The /i/ symbol and the
corresponding /u/ were introduced in the *Longman Dictionary of Contemporary English* (1987).

Another reason for differences in symbols is variation in accents. The
most obvious example is the difference between RP and the (so-called)
General American (GA) accent. The following comparison shows where
the differences lie in the vowel systems of the two accents (see Wells,
1990):

RP		GA
iː	bead	iː
ɪ	bid	ɪ
e	bed	e
æ	bad	æ
ɑː	bard	ɑːr
ɒ	cod	ɑː
ɔː	thought	ɒː
ɔː	cord	ɔː
ʊ	pull	ʊ
uː	pool	uː
ʌ	bud	ʌ
ɜː	bird	ɝː
ə	(cup)board	ə
eɪ	hay	eɪ
əʊ	hoe	oʊ
aɪ	high	aɪ
aʊ	how	aʊ
ɔɪ	boy	ɔɪ
ɪə	beer	ɪᵊr
eə	bear	eᵊr
ʊə	poor	ʊᵊr

It has also been suggested that the symbol /a/ should now be used for RP *bad* to distinguish it from GA *bad*, which has a very definite different phonetic quality.

A third reason for differences in symbols is the purpose for which they are being used. Perhaps the most obvious function of the symbols is to record simply, but unambiguously, the pronunciation of a word, or phrase, or piece of text. For this purpose, a set of symbols that represent the phonemes of the language is required, for what is known as a 'broad transcription' (technically, a 'phonemic' transcription). If, however, greater detail is required (for example to compare phonemes in two languages), then a more complicated set of symbols is required; for instance, the *r* of English *red* might need to be compared with the *r* of German *rot*, in which case [ɹ] would signify the 'frictionless continuant' or approximant /r/ of English, and [ʀ] the uvular roll of German. These more detailed symbols belong to a 'narrow transcription' (technically, a 'phonetic' or 'allophonic' transcription).

If two languages are being compared, or even two accents, some awkwardness in symbolisation can occur. /e/ is used for the vowel sound in English *bet*, but /ɛ/ is used for the almost identical vowel in German *Bett*; however, in German the symbol /e/ is needed for the vowel sound in *Beet*. For such comparative purposes, it would obviously be more sensible to use /ɛ/ for English *bet* and German *Bett*. (In this respect, Ward's and Wynn's systems, which use /ɛ/ for *bet*, are eminently more sensible; the /ɛ/ is thus conforming more closely to the international value of that symbol.)

On the other hand, if a transcription is used simply to record the pronunciation of one language without reference to any other, then the main criterion will be familiarity of symbols to the native user; and that is why most systems prefer /e/ for the *bed* vowel. (Windsor Lewis (1972) tried to promote the use of the ɒ symbol for the *cod* vowel by this argument; he succeeded in converting an earlier edition of the *Oxford Advanced Learner's Dictionary*, but otherwise failed. His use of the ɒ symbol differed markedly from the international value accorded to that symbol, and perhaps that is the reason why it did not catch on in ELT circles.)

We have now seen why it is that symbol systems can vary so. There may be theoretical reasons (e.g. Jones *vs.* Ward), changes in pronunciation, variation in accents and differences of purposes. These four reasons have been illustrated in the vowel system of English, but what about the consonants?

Fortunately, there have been no great controversies in the symbolisation of English consonants; neither have there been many historical changes. Accent variation is also less marked, and thus there has been less reason for alternative symbols. Only two points need to be made. The first is that American linguists used a number of symbols of different design, e.g.

	IPA	American
ʃ	*ship*	š
3	*measure*	ž
tʃ	*chip*	tš or č
ʤ	*major*	dž or ǰ
j	*yes*	y

The second point is that Wells highlights the phonetic differences in the *t* of British and North American *water*: /t/ for RP and /t̬/ for Americans and Canadians (see Wells, 1990:703).

Who needs the phonetic symbols and why?

Teachers need them above all, but students and learners can benefit from them, too. As was mentioned above, probably the main reason for needing phonetic symbols is for reference purposes: they provide a simple record of the pronunciation of words, phrases and pieces of text. This function appears in special pronunciation dictionaries, such as:

> Everyman's English Pronouncing Dictionary (Jones, 1977)
> Longman Pronunciation Dictionary (Wells, 1990)
> Concise Pronouncing Dictionary of British and American English (Lewis, 1972)
> An English Pronunciation Dictionary (Wynn, 1987)
> Pronouncing Dictionary of American English (Kenyon and Knott, 1953)
> BBC Pronouncing Dictionary of British Names (Pointon, 1983);

in special learner dictionaries like:

> The Oxford Advanced Learner's Dictionary of Current English (Cowie, 1989)
> The Longman Dictionary of Contemporary English (Summers, 1987)
> The COBUILD English Language Dictionary (Sinclair, 1987);

increasingly, in general dictionaries:

> Collins English Dictionary (Hanks, 1979)
> The Oxford Dictionary of Current English (Allen, 1985)
> The Oxford English Dictionary (2nd edition; Simpson and Weiner, 1989)
> The Penguin English Dictionary (1985);

and in all kinds of teaching material, textbooks, pronunciation exercise books and teachers' notes.

Teachers have debated the value of getting their learners acquainted with phonetic symbols. On the one hand, learners have enough to do without having to cope with an extra set of symbols, which are 'technical' and unfamiliar; on the other hand, learners could also benefit from the advantages that teachers themselves find in them. Underhill (1985:109) pointed out that by denying learners the opportunity of becoming familiar with them, they are denied the development of three abilities:

1   the ability to find the pronunciation and stress of any word in the dictionary;
2   the ability to record in their own handwriting the pronunciation and stress of new words, phrases, etc; and
3   the ability to objectify the string of sounds contained in a word and to study the sequences and clusters.

A fourth, general, advantage of reference to phonetic symbols is to reinforce the awareness that pronunciation learning cannot necessarily be based on spelling.

The phonetic record of the pronunciation of an English word involves not only the 'segments' (the consonants, vowels and diphthongs) but the 'suprasegments' too (word stress, or word accent, rhythm and intonation). Since word stress in English is contrastive, differences in words can be signalled solely by stress, e.g. the noun and verb forms of words like *conduct*, homographs like *invalid*, and minimal pairs like *insight* and *incite*. Word stress is also involved in rhythm, e.g. strong and weak forms of grammatical words, and changes of stress patterns as in *she's* thir**teen** and **thir**teen *years*. Word stress is conventionally indicated by small vertical marks: /'/ for primary stress, and /ˌ/ for secondary. A pause in rhythm is indicated by /ˌ/, for instance to distinguish *old men* ˄ *and women* from *old men and women*. Intonation is indicated usually by a set of accents: /'/ for rising tone, /\/ for falling, /ˆ/ for rising–falling, and /ˇ/ for falling–rising.

The discussion has so far been confined to English, where it is well known that there is a huge discrepancy between pronunciation and spelling; but a phonetic notation will also be useful for other languages where this is so. But where there is a good one-to-one correspondence, such as in Spanish, Swahili or Turkish, there is no such great necessity for phonetic notation, except, perhaps, for incidental purposes. Teachers and learners would find a phonetic notation extremely helpful where the target language does not use the roman alphabet – simply as a record of pronunciation.

A second reason for acquiring phonetic symbols is to be able to use them when discussing matters of pronunciation. Elementary introductions to linguistics and introductory guides to language teaching include them. In more technical discussions in language comparison, accent variation and historical change, phonetic symbols are taken for granted. Pedagogical materials make use of them – because they are precise, unambiguous and simple!

Phonetic transcription is another use of the symbols. Admittedly, making a transcription from written or spoken material will not necessarily improve a person's pronunciation, but it will draw attention to features of pronunciation that might easily otherwise escape notice. That is why language teachers as well as linguists are trained to transcribe:

> There is no better way to train the ear than to practise phonemic transcription and we strongly recommend that teachers try to develop

this skill. A short paragraph transcribed daily has been found to be the best method of learning the symbols, rather than sitting down and trying to memorize them en bloc. (Smith and Bloor, 1985:31)

Transcribing also makes people aware of phonetic processes like assimilation, elision, liaison, rhythm, pausing and intonation.

The fourth reason for becoming familiar with phonetic symbols is their usefulness in the classroom. Their usefulness is related directly to the preceding three purposes:

1   as a record of pronunciation;
2   as 'tools' when dealing with pronunciation issues;
3   in transcription.

How can phonetic symbols be used in the classroom?

If a teacher decides that the learners can benefit from acquaintance with the phonetic symbols, then they have to learn them. They do not need to learn them necessarily rote fashion: Underhill (1980) and James (1986) have suggested familiarisation techniques, and no doubt many a teacher has thought of imaginative ways of accomplishing this task.

Teachers will need a list of them and a set of key words. Learner dictionaries have them displayed inside the front and/or back cover; the *Longman Pronunciation Dictionary* has a detachable laminated card. Use these or invent your own, using children's names or place names, etc.: *Jean* for /iː/; *Jim* for /ɪ/; *Jenny* for /e/; *Ann* for /æ/, etc.

Some symbols are more important than others. Whereas, as a rule, /m/ and /n/ present very few problems, /θ/ and /ð/ are necessary to distinguish the two *th*'s. /s/ and /z/ are important because of the spelling problems; similarly /g/ and /dʒ/, /ʃ/ and /tʃ/, /ʒ/, and /j/ (as in *use, music*). All the vowel symbols seem to be important.

The symbols are learnt by being used, but copying, matching and sorting exercises can reinforce this. A sorting exercise can be done like this: take a number of words like *leave, live, slip, sleep, siege, sieve*, etc., and sort them into two lists.

/iː/	/ɪ/
sheep	ship

The words can be more randomly selected, for example, from a paragraph, and could be longer and more difficult, such as *routine, rhythm, sympathy, women, pizza,* etc. Completion exercises can also be used:

bread	br _ _ d
dead	d _ _ d
leaf	l _ _ f
seat	s _ _ t
break	br _ _ k

An alphabet exercise was designed by Underhill (1980) and was used in *Opening Strategies* (Abbs and Freebairn, 1982):

Puzzle

	1	2	3	4	5	6	7
Why are the letters of the alphabet arranged in these seven columns?	A	B	F	I	O	Q	R
	H	C	L	Y		U	
	J	D	M			W	
	K	E	N				
		G	S				
		P	X				
		T	Z				
	V						

1 Turn to page 1 in your dictionary.

2 Find the letter 'A', which is the first entry.

3 Notice the pronunciation /eɪ/.

Now complete this table by writing the phonetic spelling of the letters of the English Alphabet.

Check your answer by looking up each letter in your dictionary. Some of them have been completed for you.

1	2	3	4	5	6	7
A /eɪ/	B /biː/	F / /	I/ /	O/ /	Q/ /	R/ /
H /eɪtʃ/	C /siː/	L/ /	Y/ /		U/ /	
J/ /	D/ /	M/ /			W/ /	
K/ /	E/ /	N/ /				
	G/ /	S/ /				
	P/ /	X/ /				
	T/ /	Z/ /				
	V/ /					

Now practice each of the letters of the alphabet aloud, with their exact pronunciation.

(Underhill, 1980:19, by permission of Longman)

Here are two games that James (1986:39) has offered:

> *i)* '*Bingo*'
> The teacher writes 10–15 phonetic symbols/spellings on the blackboard, each of which is numbered. Some of the items are read out to the class, and the learners only jot down the corresponding numbers. The teacher checks that the class has the correct combination. (Where appropriate, this could be continued in pairs, with learners taking it in turns to read out a selection of items to each other.)
>
> *ii)* '*Kim's Game*'
> As in the 'Bingo' activity, a number of items are written on the blackboard; the learners close their eyes while the teacher rubs off one of the spellings. When asked to open their eyes, the class tries to remember what was in the space. (And so on.)

Remember that learning the phonetic alphabet is not an end in itself, and it does not directly improve pronunciation. A good spoken model is required; the symbols must be associated with accurate sounds. But once acquired, they are immensely useful, and give the learners the freedom to look up pronunciations for themselves.

Teachers can use the symbols regularly for: new words, difficult words, mispronounced words, spelling differences, word stress patterns, and idioms.

They can be used in perception/ear-training exercises. Instead of saying whether a word is '*a* or *b*', learners can identify words by /θ/ or /ð/, etc.

The symbols give teachers the freedom to use them for incidental purposes like drawing attention to pronunciation briefly when the class is primarily engaged in another activity. James (1986:41) recommends a special area of the blackboard being set aside for pronunciation.

Underhill (forthcoming) has designed what he calls a 'sound foundations phonemic chart' for use by teachers to consciously draw attention to sounds of English. You could draw up your own, but here is Underhill's:

iː	ɪ	ʊ	uː	ɪə	eɪ	ˈ, ✗
e	ə	ɜː	ɔː	ʊə	ɔɪ	əʊ
æ	ʌ	ɑː	ɒ	eə	aɪ	aʊ
p	b	t	d	tʃ	dʒ	k	g
f	v	θ	ð	s	z	ʃ	ʒ
m	n	ŋ	h	l	r	w	j

With it, teachers can remind learners of sounds and patterns (e.g. 'What is true of /t/ is true of /d/'), and get them to think of words with certain sounds, fill in gaps and even spell words in transcription. All this kind of work makes learners more aware of pronunciation and fixes it in their minds.

Is there really any point in learners transcribing words? Certainly there will be occasions when there is: 'Look, *anxious* is /ˈæŋkʃəs/ but *anxiety* is /æŋˈzaɪətɪ/', or using just the stress symbols, 'You say *adoˈlescence*, not *aˈdolescence*'. But there is another kind of transcription which learners may find useful, and that is annotating a written passage that is due to be spoken aloud. A Swedish teacher of English, Wilhelm Otnes, has devised a system of special symbols for this purpose, but if the learners already knew the phonetic alphabet, they could use those symbols instead. Here are two examples:

1. **Say what you like** (Open exercise)
Do you like pop music?   ˈmjuːzɪk
Yes, I do./No, I don't.

1	pop music?	4	your job?
2	classical music?	5	English classes?
3	cats?	6	your home town?

DIANA: Isn't it marvellous? We won. wəz

VINCE: Congratulations! The film was really great.

DIANA: Yes, I'm really pleased. We've worked on it for over two years. Let's order some champagne. And what about something to eat? Have you had lunch yet? ʃæmˈpeɪn

VINCE: No, we haven't. That sounds a good idea.

(later)

WAITER: You look happy!   əˈwɔːd

DIANA: Yes, we won a Silver Star award. Can you pour the champagne, please?

WAITER: With pleasure.

Answer:
What time of day is it?
Why is Diana happy?
Did Vince like the film?
What are they going to drink?

(Abbs and Freebairn, 1982:27, 111, by permission of Longman)

In the final analysis, teachers must decide for themselves whether to use phonetic symbols in the classroom, or not; it is a matter of assessing its desirability against such factors as time, the aim of the course, the level and age of the learners and access to dictionaries. MacCarthy reminds us:

> And again the point should be stressed that no great merit attaches to mastering a system of notation as such, but that it is only useful to the extent to which it achieves its object. (MacCarthy, 1978:31)

Haycraft encourages us about the value of phonetic symbols and adds: 'They are easy to learn' (Haycraft, 1971:95). And, finally, one of James's learners recommends:

> In my opinion it's a good system. But only if you teach it from the beginning. The new student really needs a system to remember the right pronunciation. Of course, phonetic spellings are far better than any other system invented by the learner. (James, 1986:42)

References

Abbs, B. and Freebairn, I. (1982) *Opening Strategies* Longman, Harlow.

Allen, R.E. (1985) *The Oxford Dictionary of Current English* Clarendon Press, Oxford.

Cowie, A.P. (1989) *Oxford Advanced Learner's Dictionary of Current English* Oxford University Press.

Gimson, A.C. (1962) *An Introduction to the Pronunciation of English* Edward Arnold, London. Revised by S. Ramsaran, 1989, 4th edition.

Hanks, P. (1979) *Collins Dictionary of the English Language* Collins, London.

Haycraft, B. (1971) *The Teaching of Pronunciation* Longman, Harlow.

Henderson, E.J.A. (1971) *The Indispensable Foundation: a Selection from the Writings of Henry Sweet* Longman, Harlow.

James, P. (1986) 'Sounds Useful: Helping Learners with Pronunciation', in *Modern English Teacher* 13:4, p. 36–43. Also in A. Brown (ed.) (1991) *Teaching English Pronunciation: A Book of Readings* Routledge, London p. 323–331.

Jones, D. (1975) *An Outline of English Phonetics* 9th edition, Cambridge University Press.

Jones, D. (1917) *Everyman's English Pronouncing Dictionary* Dent, London. Revised by A.C. Gimson, 1977, 14th edition.

Kenyon, J.S. and Knott, T.A. (1953) *A Pronouncing Dictionary of American English* Merriam.

Lewis, J. Windsor (1972) *A Concise Pronouncing Dictionary of British and American English* Oxford University Press.

MacCarthy, P. (1978) *The Teaching of Pronunciation* Cambridge University Press.

Otnes, W. (1969) *Signs for Sounds: English Pronunciation and Spelling Seen Together* Otnes.

Penguin (1985) *The Penguin English Dictionary* Penguin Books, Harmondsworth.

Pointon, G.E. (1983) *BBC Pronouncing Dictionary of British Names* 2nd edition, Oxford University Press.

Simpson, J.A. and Weiner, E.S.C. (1989) *The Oxford English Dictionary* 2nd edition, 20 vols. Clarendon Press, Oxford.

Sinclair, J.M. (1987) *COBUILD English Language Dictionary* Collins, London.

Smith, J. and Bloor, M. (1985) *Simple Phonetics for Teachers* Methuen, London.

Summers, D. (1987) *Longman Dictionary of Contemporary English* Longman, Harlow.

Tench, P. (1981) *Pronunciation Skills* Macmillan, Basingstoke.

Underhill, A. (1980) *Use Your Dictionary* Longman.

Underhill, A. (1985) 'Working with the Monolingual Learners' Dictionary', in R. Ilson: *Dictionaries, Lexicography and Language Learning* Pergamon/British Council, London.

Underhill, A. (forthcoming) *Sound Foundations Phonemic Chart* International House, Hastings.

Ward, I.C. (1948) *The Phonetics of English* 4th edition, Heffer, Cambridge.

Wells, J.C. (1990) *Longman Pronunciation Dictionary* Longman, Harlow.

Wynn, J.B. (1987) *An English Pronunciation Dictionary* Domino Books.

Chapter 9

Orthography: A Window on the World of Sound

Wayne B. Dickerson
University of Illinois at Urbana-Champaign

Introduction

The spelling system of English offers a remarkably transparent window on the sound system of English. It exposes the factors that are necessary to determine, among other things, the consonant and vowel constituents of words, areas of regional variation in pronunciation, and the stress and rhythm of words. The purpose of this chapter is to explore not only what orthography can reveal about phonology but also what is necessary, from a pedagogical point of view, to make these insights available to linguistically naive learners of English.

The value of spelling to learners

For learners of English, to have ready access to accurate information about the sounds of English would be like having the services of a pronunciation teacher perpetually on call. Happily, such a possibility is not mere wishful thinking; it is within the capabilities of most learners. By memorising a modest number of simple rules, adult learners can in fact become their own teachers. They can address their own basic and ongoing concerns: Am I pronouncing this word correctly? Where is its stress? Do I have the rhythm right? How does this word sound in the speech stream? Instead of looking up words for pronunciation information, they can extract that information from print. Such an ability enables learners to enlarge their speaking lexicons. More importantly, it contributes to the progress of their language learning by improving their ability to self-correct as they monitor their covertly practised speech (Dickerson, 1987).[1]

The wealth of phonological insight that teachers can make available to learners can be conveyed only if both parties appreciate the nature of English orthography and the limitations of learners to use it. Some adjustment of thinking on both sides is often necessary.

The learner's orientation

Before learners can realise the benefits of studying conventional spelling, they must come to understand some of the fundamental characteristics of English orthography. The most basic concept is that our orthography is alphabetic, that letters relate primarily to sounds, not to syllables or meanings. A surprising number of learners are unaware of the alphabetic principle. They see a spelling like *west* as a whole configuration and do not relate the *w* to /w/, or the *e* to /e/, or the *st* to /st/. This approach to English spelling, most common among those whose native orthographies are not alphabetic, is reinforced by learners' encounters with the spelling itself. Consider how arbitrary our orthography must seem to learners trying to write the /ʃ/ sound in words like *fashion, passion, facial,* and *spatial.* Since spelling seems to make so little sense when writing, can it make any more sense when reading? Many students wrongly suppose not.

Having said that our orthography is basically alphabetic, we must hasten to assert a second fundamental concept, namely, that only rarely do letters relate *directly* to sounds. Except for a half-dozen consonant spellings (*f, v, j, q, sh, z*), there are no one-to-one correlations between letters and sounds in English. Instead, letters *in a defining context* correspond to sounds; if we change the context, we often change the sound.[2] This point cautions learners against the common assumption that a stem sound in one derivative must be the same in all derivatives even though the context is different, e.g. that the *man–* of *manic* must also be /æ/ in *mania* and *maniacal.* Without this concept, learners have difficulty understanding why they are constantly asked to recognise relevant pieces of context – neighbouring vowel and consonant letters, parts of speech, prefixes and endings, positions in a word, degrees of stress, and the like.

Learners who understand the alphabetic principle and the special way that letters relate to sounds in English know where instruction is leading and participate actively to reach the goal of developing in themselves the skill to make independent judgements about the sounds of novel words.

The teacher's orientation

Unaccustomed to spelling as an important contributor to pronunciation instruction, some teachers may need to be reminded of how their linguistically unsophisticated students shape the content of pedagogical materials. Consider, for example, the learners' influence on prediction rules and the choice of transcription system.

To be easy to learn and simple to use, pedagogical rules must conform to certain learner-centred principles of design. Chief among these principles is the No-Prior-Knowledge Assumption (NPKA) (Dickerson,

1981). The application of a rule must not require learners to have prior knowledge of the language beyond a rudimentary level unless that knowledge is specifically provided during instruction. While rules may fairly expect users to recognise vowel and consonant letters and to know enough English to distinguish basic parts of speech (noun, adjective, verb, adverb), rules may not assume other knowledge about the language, such as the meaning of target words, their language of origin, their morphological composition, their pronunciation, or their uninflected forms. This point, as well as other design principles and rule characteristics, will be illustrated in the discussion of rules below.

The goal of helping learners predict sounds from spelling also affects the transcription system used in instruction. While all pedagogical symbol sets provide an internally consistent way to represent phonemes graphically, the choice of symbol set depends on one's priorities. Standardisation across publications is one priority; facilitating spelling-to-sound prediction work is another. Given the latter priority, the preferred symbol for a sound is, in principle, one drawn from spelling and associated most commonly with that sound. For instance, to predict the vowel sound in words like *west, felt, debt,* and *neck,* consider how easily the learner might gain a clue to the sound of this vowel if its symbol had the *e* shape – the shape most frequently used in spelling for that sound. By contrast, for words like *yes, yawn, yield,* and *yoke,* notice that the move from the *y* spelling to the symbol /j/ requires an extra step or rule – something like *y* = /j/ – a particularly confusing step when this same *j* shape is usually reserved for the sound in *jilt, jelly, jab,* and *June.* Similarly, in the case of these latter words, there is nothing in the shape of *j* to suggest the symbol /dʒ/. Years of classroom experience have shown that learners do best at remembering the symbols and using them to make correct predictions from spelling when they represent the /j/ sound with a symbol in the shape of *y* and the /dʒ/ sound with a symbol in the shape of *j,* shapes predominantly associated with those sounds.

Exemplar	Set 1	Set 2	Exemplar	Set 1	Set 2
see	–ē–	/iː/	cup	–u–	/ʌ/
sit	–i–	/ɪ/	fur	–ù–	/ɜː/[3]
web	–e–	/e/	ago	–ə–	/ə/
hat	–a–	/æ/	over	–ə̄–	/ə/[3]
arm	–o–	/ɑː/	page	–ā–	/eɪ/
got	–o/ô–	/ɒ/	home	–ō–	/əʊ/
saw	–o/ô–	/ɔː/	five	–ī–	/aɪ/
put	–û–	/ʊ/	out	–ou–	/aʊ/
rule	–ū–	/uː/	join	–oi–	/ɔɪ/
chin	–ch–	/tʃ/	she	–sh–	/ʃ/
June	–j–	/dʒ/	vision	–zh–	/ʒ/
yes	–y–	/j/	sing	–ng–	/ŋ/
what	–wh–	/ʍ/	thin	–th–	/θ/
			then	–TH–	/ð/

Adhering closely to the principle for selecting appropriate symbols, one set adopted for spelling-to-sound work is listed above; its symbols are placed between dashes to distinguish them from those in other sets.[3] The correspondences between the spelling-based symbols (Set 1) and those in a common set based on the International Phonetic Alphabet (Set 2) are also given. All of the vowels are listed, but consonants are listed only where differences exist between the two sets. Teachers and students who share an understanding of how English orthography works and are realistic about how to extract phonological information from written words, can move concertedly to exploit the prediction system. Some of the rules in that system can now be examined for the kinds of information they make available, as well as the learner-oriented devices they incorporate.[4] Discussed below are rules that deal with three segmental areas (consonants, vowels, and phonological variability) and two suprasegmental areas (word rhythm and word stress).

Predicting consonant sounds

The general design of most prediction rules for segmentals is captured in the statement, 'Letters *in a defining context* correspond to sounds.' They are equations in which 'letters in a defining context' are on the left of a 'correspond' symbol (=), and 'sounds' are on the right. For consonants, the rule is referred to as a *consonant-correspondence pattern* (CCP) (Dickerson, 1985).

The four words mentioned earlier that seem so enigmatic to spellers – *fashion, passion, facial,* and *spatial* – are perfectly predictable to readers; they fit CCPs of great generality, as illustrated below. Although each offers lessons on the structure of patterns in general, only two of these patterns can be examined here.[5]

| fashion | sh = –sh– | facial | c + iV = –sh– |
| passion | Cs + iV = –sh– | spatial | t + iV = –sh– |

The first pattern, sh = –sh–, is the simplest possible – a basic equation with spelling on the left and a sound prediction on the right. The *sh* has no context on the left because, as noted above, the *sh* spelling is one of the few in which a near perfect one-to-one symbol–sound correlation exists.

The second pattern, c + iV = –sh–, introduces three characteristics of CCPs. First, contextual information appears on the spelling side of the equation. +iV means 'before an iV-sequence' and is a position marker, referring to a large number of spelled strings that consist of the letter *i* followed immediately by another vowel letter (V) that is either *a, o,* or *u.* Examples are *-ia, -ial, -ian, -io, -ion, -iot, -ious, -ium,* and *-ius.* Unlike patterns such as *-cion* and *-tion,* cited in some ESL/EFL texts as cues to –sh–, the +iV notation allows CCPs to capture broad generalisations about English words and serve the learner efficiently.

Second, this pattern raises the matter of rule ordering because it is one of three patterns for the letter *c*. The +iV context distinguishes the –sh– case of *c* from the –s– case in which *c* precedes *e, y*, or any other *i*, as in *spice, spicy*, and *spicier*. The final pattern is *c* = –k–, as in *carry, scalp, brick*, and *attic*. How do the rules apply when all three spellings – *c* + iV, *ci*, and *c* – seem to fit the word *facial*? For the sake of economy, the rules have been written to apply in the order of greatest specificity to least; *c* + iV has a more specific environment than *ci*, and *ci* is more specific than *c* alone. Furthermore, the use of each rule implies the non-application of any previous rule in the *c* set. Therefore, the simplest rule on paper (*c* = –k–) is, in fact, the most complex in that it implies the absence of all more specific environments. The order of rule application, then, is the following:

$$c + iV = -sh-$$
$$ce/i/y = -s-$$
$$c = -k-$$

The third point raised by the *c* set concerns optionality – alternate environments on the left of the equation (or alternate predictions on the right). The simplest case of optionality is signalled by a slash, as in the *ce/i/y* statement, meaning that the single letter to the left of the slash can be replaced by the single letter to the right. Since only this simplest case of optionality is easy for learners to remember and use, all kinds of complex optionality, such as paired substitutions and embedded substitutions, are avoided by writing separate rules.

The most transparent correlations in English orthography between letters and sounds seem to be in the area of consonants. Yet, few of these correlations are perfect. To be interpreted, consonant letters usually require a context. A consonant-correspondence pattern provides the necessary context by information given within the pattern and by the order of the pattern within a set. The –sh– and *c* patterns have illustrated these points while introducing major rule conventions – the equation form of rules, the use of V and iV abbreviations, acceptable optionality with /, and rule ordering. Other learner-oriented conventions will surface in an examination of vowel patterns.

Predicting vowel sounds

Patterns for predicting vowel sounds from spelling are referred to as *vowel quality patterns* (VQPs) (Dickerson, 1980). Unlike CCPs that are exclusively 'specific' patterns in the sense that specific consonant spellings (left side) make specific consonant predictions (right side), VQPs may be general or specific. Wherever possible, VQPs are written as *general* patterns; the spelling component refers to a general V, meaning 'any vowel letter', and the prediction is either *long, short*, or *reduced*, capitalising on the fact that all vowels belong to one of these three general groups.[6]

The first two word lists below illustrate the basic form of a general VQP. Both contain words with short vowels that are predictable by the VQPs in the column headings. The first pattern, V́C# = short, may be read as 'a stressed vowel letter followed by a single consonant letter at the end of a word predicts a short vowel' or simply 'stressed VC end predicts short'. It illustrates the three components of a VQP – a spelling pattern (consisting of the target vowel letter (V), a relevant neighbouring letter (C), and a position marker (#)), a degree of stress (́), and a prediction (short).[7] An unstressed (̆) VC# pattern predicts a reduced vowel, as observed in the last syllable of words in the third column. The VQP illustrated in the second column, V́CC = short, consists of a stressed vowel followed by two consonant letters (even if they are identical or unspoken). More consonant letters may be present, but they are irrelevant for the prediction. In terms of rule ordering, V́C#, V̆C#, and V́CC are non-overlapping patterns and are thus not ordered with respect to each other.

V́C# = short	V́CC = short	V̆C# = reduced
whit	whistle	límĭt
not	soft	bállŏt
hum	hump	cónsŭl
shag	shack	jétsăm

The following lists draw attention to the importance of word position. All the words in these lists end in what is called a *weak ending*: *-able, -an, -ary, -e, -ed, -en, -er, -est, -ing, -ish, -or, -our, -us, -y*. The stressed VC before the weak ending predicts a long vowel in contrast to a stressed VC at the end of a word. Compare, for example, *whiter* vs. *whit*, *notable* vs. *not*, *humour* vs. *hum*. These long-vowel words fit the pattern V́C + W = long, in which +W is another position marker meaning 'before a weak ending'. (In the list, (aj) restricts the weak ending to adjectives.)

V́C + W = long

whiter	noted	shake	human
whitest	noting	shaker	humour
whitish (aj)	notable	shaky (aj)	humus
	notary	shaken	

The learner's point of view is stamped on this pattern in several important ways. First, V́C + W records a widely applicable pattern in an economical and easy-to-learn way. Second, the +W notation says that all weak endings are alike with respect to vowel prediction; no special patterns are needed for particular endings, not even the final *-e*. Third, this pattern (like other VQPs) upholds the NPKA. V́C + W applies to words in their given form; learners need not know that *white* underlies *whitish* or that *shake* underlies *shaky* in order to apply the rule. It applies to these words and to those with no underlying free stems, as in *human*.

Whether the prediction is short, long, or reduced, none of the general VQPs has yet predicted a particular vowel sound. Learners, however, need not memorise more than these patterns to arrive at a vowel prediction. Given the pedagogical symbol set and a routine called the *Symbol-Generating Mechanism*, they can create the shape and name of each target vowel, as illustrated below.

When a vowel spelling is found to match a stressed general VQP, the spelled vowel shape becomes part of the pedagogical vowel symbol, and the prediction (long or short) specifies whether the vowel symbol will have a macron or not. For example, the *ot* of *nótary* fits the V́C + W = long pattern. Therefore, the *o* spelling contributes the shape of the vowel symbol, and 'long' from the pattern prescribes the macron, creating the –ō– shape and the name Long O, as shown below. A vowel spelling that matches a short-vowel pattern offers its vowel letter shape as the symbol but without a macron. In the example below, the *ack* of *shack* fits the V́CC = short pattern, providing the shape used in –a–; 'short' and the letter name combine to form the symbol name, Short A. Finally, if the prediction is for a reduced vowel, the symbol is automatically –ə– unless the consonant after the unstressed vowel is an *r*, in which case the symbol becomes –ə̃–.[8]

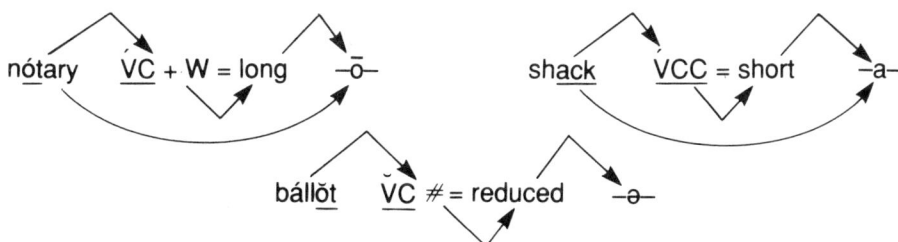

This sampling of vowel patterns has expanded the inventory of features found to be relevant for predicting sounds and introduced the notational devices to represent these features. New to this discussion is the C abbreviation for any consonant letter, the importance of degrees of stress (´ vs.˘) and word position (# vs. +W), the idea of a general pattern to capture economically the nature of English vowels, and the Symbol-Generating Mechanism to move directly from a general vowel pattern to a specific vowel symbol.

Predicting regional variation

While the orthography is extremely stable across the language, the pronunciation of educated English speakers is not.[9] In different regions, the same spellings correlate with different sounds. In many cases, CCPs and VQPs can capture regional variation for the benefit of students and teachers alike.

An example of a variable CCP comes from the +iV set previously discussed. It identifies the location of a regular difference between British and American English speech. In words fitting the rs̩ + iV = –sh/zh– pattern, illustrated below, British English speakers prefer the –sh– (/ʃ/) rendition of such words, while American English speakers tend to use the –zh– (/ʒ/) variant. Note that on the prediction side of the equation, the optionality mark (/) means that the *symbol* (not the letter) to the left can be replaced by the symbol to the right. Another difference among educated speakers is their pronunciation of the low vowel in words like *crawl* and *saw*. Language history has left some speakers preferring –o– (/ɑː/) and others using –ô– (/ɔː/). In the 'specific' VQP below, both variants are listed.

$$rs̩ + iV = -sh/zh-\qquad\qquad áw = -o/ô-$$

version	straw
excursion	drawl
Persia	yawn

Variable CCPs and VQPs together with a principled approach to variation help solve some perennially troubling problems for pronunciation teachers: What should we teach? What should we accept from our students? How can we best spend our time in class? On the assumption that students should be allowed to use the same educated variants that native speakers accept from each other, variable patterns show students and teachers where educated variation occurs. Students who know these facts are then free to select the variants that are most comfortable for them. Teachers who know the patterns can focus on the non-variable parts of the sound system and avoid inadvertently insisting on only one variant where more than one is recognised as educated English (Dickerson, 1977).

Rules with variable outputs illustrate for the prediction side of the equation what has already been noted for the spelling side, namely, simple optionality using the / device. In the –sh/zh– case, the prediction is for *s* alone, as marked by _..._ . When learners understand that the classroom approach to variation gives them greater options, the presence of variants in a few of their patterns is appreciated.

Predicting word rhythm

Our attention now turns to suprasegmentals, particularly word rhythm and word stress (accent). To the extent that standard orthography exposes the criteria governing suprasegmentals, it can serve students who want to improve their English in these areas. The first illustration concerns a piece of the basic rhythm pattern regulating English words.

Phonologists note that the vowel in a word-initial syllable preceding the stressed vowel (pretonic) will be full or reduced depending on syllable structure (Chomsky & Halle, 1968:242(24); Kreidler, 1989:236; Dickerson, 1989a, Unit 3:111–120). As the first column below demonstrates, the vowel in an initial-pretonic or *initial-prestress* syllable is a full vowel if two different consonant letters follow the vowel letter. The next two columns show that an initial-prestress vowel is reduced if the spelling is a VC or VC2 (two identical consonant letters.)[10] This group of reduced-vowel spellings is in the majority and promotes the alternating, reduced-full vowel rhythm so characteristic of English words.

VCC	VC	VC2	IP Prefix
plantátion	stabílity	battálion	advísory
lymphátic	vicínity	millénium	inspécted
vestígial	phenómenal	felónious	restríct
pontíficate	monógamous	posséssive	compúlsive

The clear distinction that separates a 'true' VCC from a VC or VC2 justifies a group label for the reduced-vowel set; for instructional purposes, the group is referred to by its position as the IP (initial-prestress) set. The label makes it possible to summarise the reduced-vowel phenomenon in a VQP: ĬP = reduced.

The distinction between true VCCs and IP spellings seems to fade, however, when a prefix is in IP position. Consider the words in the last column above where the prefixes form true VCC syllables. Although reduced vowels occur in all of these prefix syllables, they are not anomalies. Instead, another valuable generalisation has surfaced: a prefix in IP position has a reduced vowel no matter what kind of spelling pattern it creates with its stem.[11] Stated as a VQP, the pattern is ĬPP = reduced, where IPP stands for 'initial-prestress prefix' (Dickerson, 1989a, Unit 2:74). Being more specific than ĬP = reduced, this pattern takes precedence in the order of application.

Fortunately for learners who want to concentrate on their word rhythm, English orthography not only reveals the difference between types of syllable structure but also preserves the distinction between non-prefix and prefix syllables. Given that Anglo-Saxon and Latin-origin prefixes are readily identifiable in English words, learners can use the VCC, IP, and IPP patterns for nearly any word they encounter. The importance of prefix identification and word position also appears in the following discussion of word stress.

Predicting word stress

Word stress in English, which is neither marked in standard orthography nor uniformly located on words, often poses a serious problem for learners. So many characteristics of word- and phrase-level phonology are contingent on word stress that stress errors often have devastating effects on intelligibility. For this reason, many students need special help predicting word stress, an area in which conventional orthography can play an important role.

To exemplify the utility of spelling for purposes of stress assignment and to highlight again the fundamental importance of the No-Prior-Knowledge Assumption, this discussion focuses on words ending in -*able*. The analysis will also bring to light additional features, accessible through orthography, that bear on the prediction of word-level phonology.

A common approach to -*able* among stress researchers is to distinguish between an -*able* attached to an independent word and an -*able* attached to a non-independent stem (e.g. Guierre, 1984:35, 121; Kreidler, 1989:312). In the first case, -*able* is ignored and the free stem is stressed as it would be without the suffix. In the second case, the bound stem is analysed.

To those familiar with English, this approach may seem perfectly workable. However, examined from the viewpoint of learners of English, the strategy fails because it ignores the NPKA. In particular, it relies unfairly on the learners' knowledge of English to distinguish independent from non-independent stems. Consider the problems that learners face with the bulk of -*able* words, namely, those that have no internal suffixes, as illustrated below.

acceptable	regrettable	memorable	delectable
governable	practicable	pulverable	vulnerable
distinguishable	revocable	tolerable	amicable
unanswerable	fatigable	inflammable	indomitable

Most learners will probably recognise stems in the first column as free-standing words. But is *unanswer-* really a free stem? In the second column, more ambiguities surface. The *t* of *regrettable* is doubled; is *regrett* an independent stem? In *practicable*, the final *e* is missing from *practice*. Does the remainder qualify as a word? Is the *revoc-* of *revocable* a free stem? Learners may think of *revoke*, but the *k*-to-*c* change and the loss of a final *e* may make them wonder. Learners might be reminded of *fatigue* when looking at *fatigable*, but does this -*able* word have an independent stem? Similarly, items in the third column may hint at familiar stems – *memory*, *pulverise*, *tolerate*, and *inflame*. But those in the last column suggest no obvious free-stem origins. The gradation between an entirely transparent stem and an entirely opaque stem is full of 'ifs, ands, and buts', uncomfortable, if not impossible, territory for learners to traverse.

In the end, do learners have to know the language in order to learn it? Such a demand violates the NPKA because it taxes learners beyond reason. From the point of view of stress placement, is it necessary? Must the stressing strategy be different for *acceptable* and *delectable*? The answer is, no; it need not be different.

The Prefix Weak Stress Rule (PWSR) (Dickerson, 1989a, Unit 2:97–

106) applies to certain classes of verbs and to words with Prefix Weak endings, of which *-able* is one. The rule asks learners to identify the spelled syllable left of *-able* as the *Key Syllable* or starting point for the analysis. The Key Syllable is underlined in the words above. Learners then must examine the spelled syllable to the left of the Key, the *Left Syllable*. As examples, the Left Syllable in the first word of each column is, respectively, *acc*, *egr*, *em*, and *el*. Next they must answer this question: Does the Left Syllable contain any part of a prefix? If so, the stress goes on the Key Syllable, if not, the stress goes on the Left Syllable. The PWSR is stated below.

PREFIX WEAK STRESS RULE

From the Key, Stress Left but not a Prefix.

If you can't Stress Left, Stress Key.

With a single approach that does not violate the NPKA, the PWSR leads to the correct stress for the *-able* words above, including one of the two educated pronunciations of *revocable*.[12]

By the time students discover this rule, they can be well prepared to use it. In their study of vowel quality patterns, they can also learn to identify Key Syllables. Furthermore, their work on word rhythm can introduce them to Anglo-Saxon and Latinate prefixes so they can recognise prefixes in Left Syllables, such as the *ac-* prefix in *acc* and part of the *re-* and *de-* prefixes in *egr* and *el* in the words above.

The case of *-able* is but one illustration of how orthography can contribute significantly to a learner's control over word stress. The phonological and morphological structures of English words are represented so clearly in spelling that relevant positions such as the Key and Left Syllables, as well as the presence or absence of prefixes, can be determined with great accuracy. The result, as illustrated, is that learners can assign word stress without drawing on their knowledge of the English lexicon to judge the independence of stems.[13]

Treatment of exceptions

The segmental and suprasegmental rules illustrated above, as well as all other spelling-based patterns, while extremely accurate predictors, are not perfectly accurate. In some cases, more specific patterns capture minor regularities, but still irregularities remain. Several factors are responsible for them. They arise in part from the fact that the language is not entirely regular. Language change and foreign borrowings create anomalies for any rule system. Exceptions also arise in part from inconsistencies in our ancient spelling system. This is particularly the case for vowel spellings among the most common words in the English lexicon. Finally, erroneous predictions arise in part from the rules themselves – from the criteria they employ and their specificity.[14]

As a fact of language and language rules, exceptions should be dealt with in a straightforward manner. Experience offers these suggestions. Teachers should tell students explicitly how accurate the rules are. Since rules of the kind discussed above have predictive accuracies above 95 per cent, the information helps students understand the power they gain by learning rules even when there are exceptions. The alternative to rules should also be pointed out, namely, the gargantuan task of memorising word-by-word the pronunciation of all the words to which the rules apply. The information about accuracy also serves notice that the pronunciation of a small percentage of words is mispredicted. The most common of these exceptions should be listed for students to learn. Having learned them, students not only know how to pronounce the words that cannot be predicted by rule but also can apply their rules to the remaining words with the confidence that they will make correct predictions.

Conclusion

Whether learners are interested in segmentals or suprasegmentals, they can access a great deal of relevant information through ordinary English spelling without the prerequisite of prior proficiency in the language. Although this chapter has not exhausted the kinds of information that can be derived from spelling, it has examined a range of sound-system phenomena and illustrated the kind of transcription system, rules, and rule characteristics that facilitate sound-system predictions.[15]

Implicit in this discussion has been the assumption that pronunciation instruction should consist of more than pronouncing and listening to pronunciations. Indeed, to limit learners to production and perception activities is to impose on them the handicap of being unable to make reliable judgements about the sounds of words and phrases they may not have seen before. The skill of prediction does not come naturally; therefore it should be added as an explicit goal of all pronunciation instruction and integrated thoroughly into the work done on all pronunciation topics. To the extent possible, all literate learners should have the opportunity to look for themselves at the inner workings of English phonology through the ever-present window of English orthography.

Notes

1   The use of orthography as a self-monitoring tool has great potential for learners in non-English speaking parts of the world where native-speaker models may not be available. In large classes where oral/aural work is difficult, if not impossible,

prediction work offers an activity that can develop learners into independent self-teachers.

2   For a discussion of how English orthography works, common misconceptions, and prerequisites for successful spelling reform, see Dickerson (1989a, Unit 3:141–146).

3   The pedagogical symbols introduced here bear many similarities to those found in some English dictionaries. A presentation of these symbols can be found in Dickerson (1989a, Unit 1:11–30), and an explanation in Dickerson (1989b, Unit 1:5–9). Of particular interest are the symbols –ù– and –ə̀–. Unlike the other symbols, each of these represents a range of articulations. The 'dotted' vowels represent mid-central vowels (stressed and unstressed, respectively) before a spelled *r*, an environment in which regional pronunciations vary from a heavily retroflexed to a non-retroflexed articulation, with vowel lengthening in some cases. If the *r* is pronounced, it is transcribed with –r–, e.g. –mùrdər–; if it is not pronounced, it is not transcribed, e.g. –mùdə̀–.

4   As the discussion progresses, it will become increasingly obvious why the pedagogical approach to spelling must be through a cohesive system rather than through a miscellany of rules. Serving the learner and the teacher best, the system approach provides the necessary consistency of rule form, notational conventions, terminology, assumptions about background knowledge and preparation, use of transcription symbols, and integration of segmental and suprasegmental rules. Repeated reference is made to the author's work primarily because, at the moment, it is the most comprehensive pedagogical prediction system for pronunciation yet available.

5   For a comprehensive look at +iV patterns, see Dickerson (1989a, Unit 2:59–68); for s + iV patterns in the context of other *s* patterns, see Dickerson (1990a:51).

6   An example of a 'specific' VQP is given in the next section on regional variation. While a general VQP has a general V and a general prediction, a specific pattern has a specific component on one or both sides of the equation (Dickerson, 1989a, Unit 1:99).

7   Since stress is one component of a VQP, the stress of a target word must be known before a VQP can be used (but see note 10 below). In most cases, word stress is predictable. Although unmarked, major stress (´) is considered part of every monosyllabic word in isolation. The stress of polysyllabic words is assigned by learner-friendly rules, such as the one illustrated below.

8   For a survey of the most productive VQPs in English, including patterns with postvocalic *r*, see Dickerson (1989a, Unit 1, Chapter 2). The workings of the Symbol-Generating Mechanism are described in Dickerson (1989a, Unit 1:159).

9   For a contrast of British and American spelling practices, see Dickerson (1989a, Unit 1:152–154). Emery (1973) renders a service with his compilation of variant spellings found in five major American English dictionaries. Variants in British spelling are also fully represented because the dictionaries cover British usage as well.

10 Also in this set are Vr, Vr2, VCr, and VCl spellings (Dickerson, 1989a, Unit 3:114). Before using patterns for short and reduced vowels, learners apply patterns that predict long vowels (Dickerson, 1989a, Unit 3:99–110). Even though all VQPs include a stress component (´ , ` , ˘), it is important to understand a difference between vowel prediction in Key and Left Syllables and vowel prediction in syllables left of the major stress. To make predictions for Key and Left Syllables, major stress must be assigned first. The spelling and stress configuration is then matched to a VQP. To predict vowels left of the major stress, the stress of those syllables need not be determined before using the VQP. Instead, the pattern is matched to the spelling alone. Once matched, the VQP predicts the vowel sound and the stress.

11 A more careful formulation of this generalisation would limit its application to *merged* prefixes (Dickerson, 1989a, Unit 2:4, 73). Merged prefixes have lost their

distinctive connotations and no longer contribute explicitly to the meaning of a word, unlike *neutral* prefixes that carry obvious semantic weight. Compare the items in these merged-neutral pairs: *debate* vs. *debug*, *prepared* vs. *prepasted*, and *received* vs. *resealed*. In most cases, merged prefixes attach to non-independent stems, while neutral prefixes attach to independent stems.

Although the definition of merged and neutral prefixes involves lexical meaning, learners do not have to use meaning to distinguish these types of prefixes; instead, structural and other clues serve in all cases except for some instances of *de-*, *pre-*, *re-*, *pro-*, *co-*, *in-* ['not'], *dis-*, *ex-*, and *sub-*. A pedagogical presentation of merged and neutral Anglo-Saxon and Latin-origin prefixes, including the difficult cases, is given in Dickerson (1989a, Unit 2, Chapter 1).

12   For a full analysis of *-able*, see Dickerson (1989a, Unit 2:152–53; Unit 3:158–59, 170). In the PWSR, the phrase 'If you can't Stress Left' accommodates not only cases in which part of a prefix is in the Left Syllable but also cases in which there is no Left Syllable, as in *notable, culpable, likeable*, and *affable*.

13   The complete word-stress system presented to high-intermediate and advanced learners of English in Dickerson (1989a) consists of four simple stress rules that apply to some 70,000 words. Depending on the word class, predictive accuracy ranges between 95 per cent and 99 per cent. Furthermore, students learn to predict all the vowels in all the words they can stress.

14   The tension for applied linguists is to write pedagogical rules that walk the line between being overly detailed for the sake of improved accuracy and overly general for the sake of learnability. The rule with many conditions is hard to learn and use, while the rule that is oversimplified yields many exceptions that must be memorised. Resolution of this tension comes with the real-world use and testing of rules in ESL/EFL instruction.

15   In other areas, too, orthography can add to learners' accuracy and self-monitoring capabilities. For example, the selection of allomorphs of the troublesome {Z} and {D} morphemes can be significantly streamlined by taking a visual rather than an aural approach (Dickerson, 1990c). Furthermore, the many devices that speakers use to squeeze and smooth the speech stream to maintain the regular beat of phrase rhythm are accessible through standard spelling (Dickerson, 1990b).

References

Chomsky, N. and Halle, M. (1968) *The Sound Pattern of English* Harper & Row, New York.

Dickerson, W. (1977) 'The problem of dialects in teaching pronunciation' in *English Teaching Forum* 15:2, 18–21.

Dickerson, W. (1981) 'Bisyllabic laxing rule: Vowel prediction in linguistics and language learning' in *Language Learning* 31:1, 283.

Dickerson, W. (1981) 'A pedagogical interpretation of generative phonology: II. The main word stress rules of English, in *TESL Studies* 4, 57–93.

Dickerson, W. (1985) 'The visible Y: A case for spelling in pronunciation learning' in *TESOL Quarterly* 19:2, 303–316.

Dickerson, W. (1987) 'Orthography as a pronunciation resource' in *World Englishes* 6:1, 11–20. Also in A. Brown (ed.) (1991) *Teaching English Pronunciation: A Book of Readings* Routledge, London, 159–172.

Dickerson, W. (1989a) *Stress in the Speech Stream: The Rhythm of Spoken English. Student Text* University of Illinois Press.

Dickerson, W. (1989b) *Stress in the Speech Stream: The Rhythm of Spoken English. Teacher's Manual* University of Illinois Press.

Dickerson, W. (1990a) 'English ⟨s⟩: Cracking a symbol-sound code' in *Issues and Developments in English and Applied Linguistics* 5, 39–64.

Dickerson, W. (1990b) 'It's about time ... and timing: The consequences of English rhythm' paper presented at the 1990 Midwest TESOL Conference, St Paul, Minnesota.

Dickerson, W. (1990c) 'Morphology via orthography: A visual approach to oral decisions' in *Applied Linguistics* 11:3, 238–252.

Emery, D. (1973) *Variant Spellings in Modern American Dictionaries* (rev. ed.). National Council of Teachers of English.

Guierre, L. (1984) *Drills in English Stress-Patterns* (4th ed.) Armand Colin-Longman.

Kreidler, C. (1989) *The Pronunciation of English* Basil Blackwell, Oxford.

Chapter 10
Making Pronunciation Visible

Jonathan Marks
International House, Munich

Introduction

Among the components of a language teaching programme, pronunciation is the one which, because of its focus on the way language *sounds*, might seem most logically to demand a purely oral/aural treatment. But this would be an extreme position to adopt, for at least two reasons.

Firstly, users of many languages, including English, have found it expedient to adopt an agreed system for the visual representation of elements of pronunciation. This is the origin of alphabets and punctuation, which enable language users to record, transmit and perpetuate instances of language performance independently of human memory systems, and to encode new instances for similar processing. Knowledge of the relationships between these spoken and written forms is an important aspect of knowledge of a language.

Secondly, sounds are fleeting, but in the teaching/learning process it is important to be able to freeze them into a permanently available repertoire of symbols for reference, comment, comparison, practice, correction and recombination. The conventional written form of the language is an obvious first place to look for such a repertoire. In English, we find that phonemes are represented with varying consistency by alphabet letters and combinations of these; for example, /m/ is represented fairly consistently by the letter *m*, while *schwa* is represented much less consistently. Some features of intonation are represented partially by punctuation conventions. In contrast, word stress and phonetic, as opposed to phonemic, information are often not represented at all.

Consistency in the representation of phonemic and phonetic information for teaching purposes can be achieved through the use of transcriptions; however, this chapter will concern itself with other ways of making stress, intonation and segmental phonology visible for teaching purposes. In so doing, it will focus on some of the benefits to be derived by the pronunciation teacher from the use of Cuisenaire rods.

Cuisenaire rods

Cuisenaire rods, named after their Belgian inventor, are a set of blocks of wood with straight edges and uniform 1cm square cross-section, but of 10 different lengths, ranging from 1cm to 10cm (so that the shortest is, strictly speaking, a cube). Each of the 10 lengths has its own colour. They were originally devised for the teaching of mathematics; their usefulness to the teacher of language extends far beyond the realm of pronunciation, and no doubt they have applications in many other spheres of education, too.

Making word stress visible

In writing on the board and in producing their own written teaching materials, teachers use various conventions for marking stressed syllables within words, including the following:

1   pho*to*graphy

2   pho'tography

3   phoTOgraphy

4   pho**to**graphy

     O
5   photography

   o O o   o
6   photography

All of these have their strengths and weaknesses. No. 2 has the virtue of familiarising learners with the kind of convention to be found in most dictionaries (although the Cobuild dictionary uses a combination of nos. 1 and 4), but may be regarded as not sufficiently striking in its visual impact, and does not, to the untutored eye, locate stress unambiguously. No. 3 may have a powerful impact for learners who are very familiar with the Latin alphabet, but may appear confusing to those who are not. What is most important, though, is that whatever convention is chosen is used consistently, so that it quickly becomes part of the unambiguous shared 'language' of the class.

Nos. 5 and 6 suggest another principle for visually representing stress, namely that the spelling of the word, whether orthographic or phonemic/phonetic, does not need to be given if such information is redundant to the issue being worked on. Instead, the following types of convention may be used (again, the example word is *photography*):

7   oOoo

8   o●oo

9   −+−−

Syllables represented in this way can also be freed from a writing surface such as blackboard or paper. Shapes like o and O can be cut out of card (or represented by coins of different sizes) and learners and teachers can easily move them around a table or other horizontal surface in order to test hypotheses, compare different stress patterns, or correct stress placement. Such an arrangement can also be projected on an OHP or stuck to a vertical surface using Blu-tak or some similar temporary adhesive. The use of a vertical surface may of course be preferable for the sake of visibility, particularly in large classes.

Three-dimensional symbols can be used in exactly the same way, and Cuisenaire rods lend themselves particularly well to this role. They are ready-made objects which can also be used for numerous other purposes in the classroom. Apart from their dimensions and colours, they are completely devoid of their own 'content', which allows them to represent very purely whatever content is invested in them by classroom conventions. They also seem to invite people to pick them up and play with them. They are equally flexible with regard to the options for modes of display noted above. In work on stress, a suitable convention might be that a light green rod (3cm long) represents an unstressed syllable and a yellow one (5cm long) represents a stressed one.

For example, different groups in the class can be asked to predict the stress pattern of a word encountered in a written context, and to present their predictions to each other visually using rods. In order to do this, they must decide first how many syllables there are in the word, and therefore how many rods are needed, and then how they should be arranged. A next step might be for someone in the class, or perhaps the teacher, to say the word in all the suggested ways and for the class to 'vote' on which version they think is right. The correct version of *photography* could be represented by any of the following arrangements:

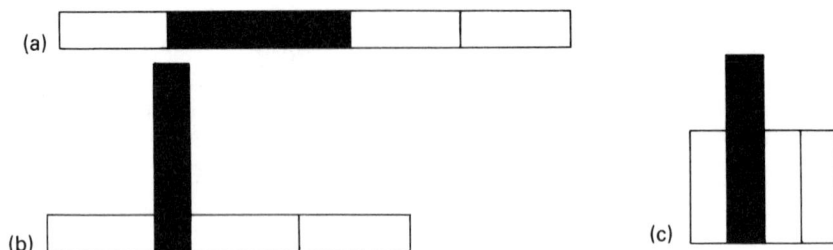

A way of representing word stress which combines the use of auditory, visual and kinaesthetic channels is tapping, clapping or stamping the rhythm of the word, with a strong stroke for the stressed syllable(s) and weak ones for the rest.

Making intonation visible

The same principles as above can apply to the representation of features of intonation. The melody of speech can be drawn as a continuous line above a written utterance on the board or on paper, or it can be drawn by a hand in the air in parallel with its spoken realisation. Or, depending on the exact focus of teaching, it may be considered sufficient to apply these lines and gestures not to the whole utterance but only to the melodic movements of tonic prominences.

Cuisenaire rods can also function as line drawings to represent intonation. For example, a realisation of *What are you doing?* with a fall on *doing* could look something like this:

In teaching intonation, however, it may sometimes be unnecessary, or even undesirable, to work explicitly on the *direction* of pitch movements, for the following reasons:

1. For some groups of learners, and some individuals, appropriate *placement* of tonic prominence automatically brings with it an appropriate *melodic* component. No doubt this is due, when it occurs, in large part to congruity between intonation patterns in L1 and L2, as well as, perhaps, an intuitive 'ear' for the Englishness of English intonation. In this case, in order to prompt a melodically appropriate realisation, it will be sufficient to locate tonic prominence. Thus, *What are you doing?* could be represented as follows:

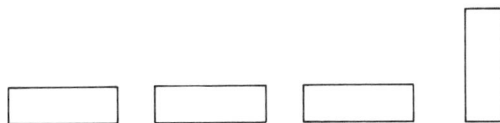

Whether or not this is adequate in particular cases can only be determined by trial and error.

2. Some learners – and more than a few teachers – cannot identify the direction of pitch movements accurately. Insistence on exercises which highlight the ability to do so may be extremely demotivating in such cases. But the majority of listeners are probably able, much more reliably, to judge whether two given melodic movements are the same or different. This is the basis for working through a minimal-pair procedure and setting up a classroom convention of pitch movements

labelled not 'fall', 'fall–rise' and so on, but simply 'A', 'B' and so on, or whatever other terminology suggests itself. (The number of terms needed will depend on the pedagogic model of intonation the teacher is working with; I am assuming here that it will not be more than three or four.) In this case, the different pitch movements can be shown by different coloured rods. Indeed, the colours can become the 'names' of the movements.

Tonic prominence placement can also be indicated by using gesture to beat the rhythm of an utterance in the same way as was suggested earlier for word stress. The use of gestures involving the hands, head or whole body in parallel with the placement of prominent syllables can be studied on video, making use of a variety of sound-off and sound-on options for prediction, identification and practice.

Making phonemes visible

Cross-sectional diagrams through the head, showing the positions of the speech organs, are a well-known means of representing the articulation of the sounds of a language. There is no reason why such diagrams should not be used for foreign-language teaching purposes, provided learners, most of whom cannot be assumed to have any training in phonetics, are given adequate guidance as to how to interpret them. Three-dimensional *models* of the head may be clearer for some learners than diagrams.

Features of articulation which are visible from the outside, particularly those involving the lips, can be modelled, and even exaggerated, by the teacher, either in conjunction with the actual realisation of the sound concerned, or silently. The silent option has the advantage of focusing attention, without the distraction of sound, on visible features which may help learners to approximate more closely to acceptable articulations. Such features include lip-rounding for /uː, w, ʃ, r/, contact between upper teeth and lower lip for /f/ and /v/, openness for /æ/ and /ɑː/, and increasing closure with duration for /əʊ/ as opposed to static setting with duration for /ɔː/. This principle of modelling can be used to introduce unfamiliar sounds or to guide learners to improve their articulation of known ones.

There is also scope for the use of video in the study of visible features of articulation. The look of certain sounds, along the same lines as the examples above, can be identified and perhaps compared with learners' own realisation of them; here a video recording facility is obviously useful, but a mirror can also play the role of a feedback mechanism. Lip-reading, with the teacher or the learners silently mouthing sounds or words, can also help to foster awareness of the look of sounds, and the physical movements needed to produce the look.

Features of length can be represented by gestures drawn in the air. Long vowel sounds can be drawn out – and here again there may be a role for exaggeration – over several feet, while short ones are compressed into a couple of inches. These gestures can accompany articulation of the sound in question, or they may be used as silent prompts for learners to improve their performance.

Cuisenaire rods can represent phonemes too. A convention can be set up involving, say, five different coloured rods to represent different sounds. For example:

white	(1cm)	= /ə/
red	(2cm)	= /b/
green	(3cm)	= /r/
pink	(4cm)	= /t/
yellow	(5cm)	= /aɪ/

One possible exercise would be for groups of learners, each with a 'pool' of rods, to construct as many words as possible, e.g. *tie, bite, try, buy*. They can then spell them as well, e.g. /raɪt/ = *right, write*, in order to help develop their awareness of English words as combinations of a limited set of units, and of relationships between sound and spelling. Just a couple of the many possibilities with the above set are given below.

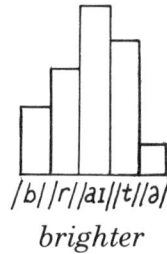

/t//r//aɪ/

try

/b//r//aɪ//t//ə/

brighter

Rods which represent sounds in this way can be moved together in order to indicate linking between words:

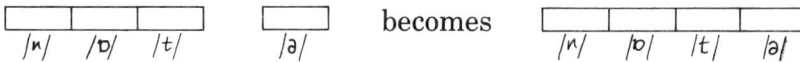

/n/ /ɒ/ /t/   /ə/   becomes   /n/ /ɒ/ /t/ /ə/

not a (in a phrase like *not a good idea*).
Rods can be taken away to indicate elision:

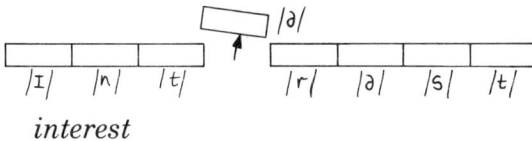

/ə/

/ɪ/ /n/ /t/   /r/ /ə/ /s/ /t/

interest

They can be superimposed to indicate assimilation:

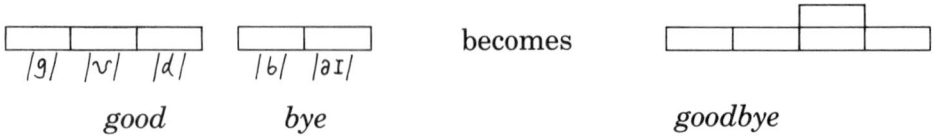

$/g/$ $/ʊ/$ $/d/$ $/b/$ $/aɪ/$ becomes

good   *bye*   *goodbye*

Cuisenaire rods are a flexible addition to the range of options open to the teacher who wishes to make pronunciation visible. It seems sensible to explore as many ways as possible of increasing this range, so that we can offer as many routes as possible for learners to build an awareness of the nature of English pronunciation.

Note

Cuisenaire rods are available from the following suppliers:

Educational Solutions
95 University Place
New York
NY10003–4555
USA

Educational Solutions (UK) Ltd.
11 Crown St.
Reading
RG1 2TQ
UK

Chapter 11
Head Diagrams

Adam Brown
The British Council, Singapore

Introduction

Gilbert (1978) argues that, while oral/aural exercises and materials are of obvious importance in pronunciation teaching, any teacher who relies solely on such materials is underusing the resources available to her. In particular, she points to psychological studies which have shown that language is centred in the left side of the brain.

> For practical classroom purposes, I think it is useful to think of the right brain/left brain contrast as the difference between verbal and non-verbal learning. The most productive teaching would seem to be that which appeals to *both* sides of the brain. (Gilbert, 1978:68)

Gilbert's article contains several suggestions for enjoyable classroom activities in which the right, non-verbal side of the brain is brought into use in pronunciation teaching. Other methods which can be employed include head diagrams. They are regularly used in phonetics courses, and several books on pronunciation teaching also include them.

Pronunciation teaching methodology

Strevens (1974) draws a useful distinction concerning the kind of information presented to learners in pronunciation teaching. This takes the form of a dichotomy between two principles (he calls them 'rival virtues'). The first is defined as follows:

> Most learners will learn to produce most sound features of a foreign language with reasonable accuracy by mimicry alone, given the opportunity; this ability tends to decrease with age. (Strevens, 1974:185)

This is called the *Innocence Principle*. It is contrasted with the *Sophistication Principle*:

> Older learners can derive more benefit than younger learners from formal, intellectualised teaching methods; the more sophisticated the learner, the more sophisticated the instruction that can be used, and the

higher the standard of achievement per hour of instruction he will typically reach. (Strevens, 1974:187)

There are many learners, including adults, who find a descriptive approach to the teaching of pronunciation unhelpful, and who would prefer simple mimicry of model sounds. The following quotation from Jerome K. Jerome's *Three Men on the Bummel* is anecdotal, but illustrates this attitude well.

> I ... think the pronunciation of a foreign tongue could be better taught than by demanding from the pupil those internal acrobatic feats that are generally impossible and always useless. This is the sort of instruction one receives. 'Press your tonsils against the underside of your larynx. Then with the convex part of the septum curved upwards so as almost but not quite to touch the uvula, try with the tip of your tongue to reach your thyroid. Take a deep breath and compress your glottis. Now, without opening your lips, say "Garoo"'. And when you have done it they are not satisfied. (Jerome, 1900, quoted by Kenworthy, 1987:69)

Head diagrams are clearly a sophisticated form of instructional aid. They are less likely to prove effective in the teaching of young learners, and many adults may also find them confusing rather than illuminating. Nevertheless, with more sophisticated learners they are another useful weapon in the ELT instructor's arsenal.

Cant (1976) is one of the few writers to have discussed the place of head diagrams, along with other visual aids such as phonetic symbols, in pronunciation teaching. He proposes four features for effective courses, even at beginner level:

1 the terminology is kept as simple and obvious as possible;
2 a special transcription is avoided, and practice lists are given in the orthography;
3 the phonetic information is presented in diagrams which may be related together by brief descriptive notes; and
4 the programming enables the learner to acquire the phonetic information in a systematic way, and thus develop direction and control of his performance as rapidly as possible. (Cant, 1976:300)

He concludes by saying that 'the only general rule governing all diagrams is that they should be as simple and obvious as possible' (Cant, 1976:301). To this we might add that, while being diagrammatic, they should not be inaccurate in relation to the physiological facts.

There are three ways of dividing the head in head diagrams. The commonest, which divides the head left from right, is known as a *sagittal* section. One which divides the head front from back is known as a *coronal* section. The final type, dividing the head top from bottom, is a *transverse* section.

Inaccuracies of head diagrams

Many of the head diagrams which have been published in books on phonetics and pronunciation teaching are seriously inaccurate in certain anatomical and physiological respects.

If you put the tip of your tongue on your lower teeth, and move it downwards, you can easily feel that there is a deep trough inside the front of the mouth extending a good deal of the way down towards the chin. This is usually missing in head diagrams.

It might be objected that there is a web of the underside of the tip of the tongue which lies in the mid plane. Strictly speaking then, it is accurate that this is what is shown in a sagittal section. However, it should be noted that this web is quite insubstantial and does not severely restrict the movement of the tongue. It is quite possible, for example, to pull the tip of the tongue a long way back from the lower front teeth. This can be easily verified in a mirror.

Similarly, the mid section of the nose is composed of cartilage, called the *septum*. However, head diagrams normally show the nose as a large cavity. It is true that the nose contains two large cavities (the nostrils), but these do not occur in the mid plane.

Likewise, when students study head diagrams in books, they often overlook the fact that the teeth and alveolar ridge are not located solely at the front of the mouth, but extend in a U shape around the sides.

Gilbert (1978:71) suggests that the two-dimensional nature of head diagrams can be easily overcome by buying a three-dimensional plaster model, of the kind commonly found in hospitals. This may be larger than life-size, and therefore usable in classrooms. The various parts are movable, and students can therefore get a more comprehensive picture of the articulation of sounds than that afforded by head diagrams.

Two further points are important and patently obvious when pointed out, but are nevertheless often overlooked by the designers of head diagrams. The first is that the jaw moves up and down, and adopts different degrees of openness for the different sounds. This is most important for vowels. One of the main differences in the articulation of vowels like [iː] and [æ] is the openness of the jaw. Textbooks normally refer instead to the height/lowness of the tongue. However, this is often difficult for students to appreciate (see *Tongue contact* below). It is important to remember that the tongue is attached to the jaw, and tends to work hand-in-hand with it. It is, for example, very difficult or at least awkward to produce an [iː] with the jaw in the open position typical for [æ], and vice versa. Students' attention is therefore better drawn to the easily seen position of the jaw rather than the hidden position of the tongue. It is also worth noting here that the degree of lip-rounding tends to be associated with the closeness of the jaw. It is, for example, very difficult to produce the lip-rounding of [uː] with the jaw in the open position typical of [ɑː] (see *Lip-rounding* below).

The second point is that the tongue is not a small organ. It is a bundle of muscles which fills a substantial proportion of the oral cavity and can assume an enormous number of different positions. Again, this can be easily verified in a mirror. In some head diagrams, it is simply drawn too small and is reminiscent of a pet parrot's.

The following diagrams are taken from Baker (1981) but are typical of many pronunciation and phonetics textbooks in their inaccuracies. Note the following:

1   There is no space below the tip of the tongue.
2   The jaw position remains the same for all five vowels.
3   The same vowels are given differing tongue positions, depending on the positions of the other vowel being contrasted.

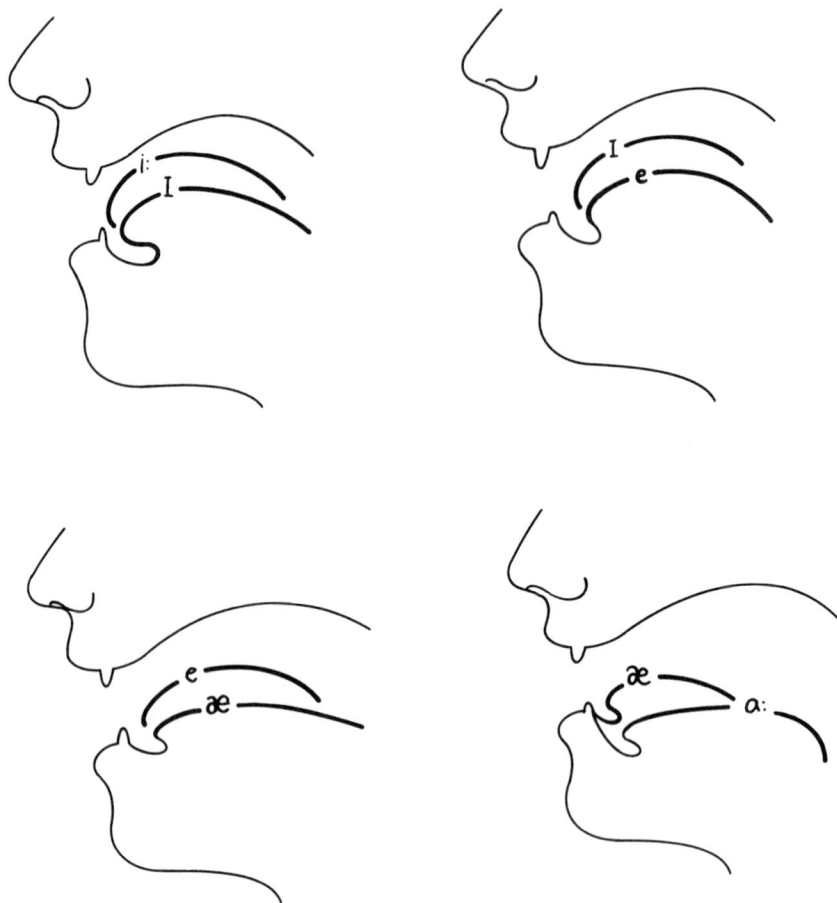

Figure 1   Sagittal sections for [iː, ɪ, e, æ, ɑː] (from Baker, 1981:6, 9, 12, 19)

Inaccuracies such as these can be avoided by basing head diagrams on X-ray photographs of the head. This is precisely what better phonetics books do, e.g. Ladefoged (1982). The OHP diagram at the end of this chapter is based on a diagram from Laver (1980:24) which is itself traced from an X-ray.

Another small point is that published diagrams seem to be chauvinistically male. One advantage of this is that male larynxes, being physically larger than females', are more conducive to diagrammatic representation. One exception to this trend is the diagram in Fromkin and Rodman (1978:68).

Limitations of head diagrams

There are several limitations to head diagrams. In certain cases, they are simply incapable of showing particular features; in others, they should be used in conjunction with other sorts of diagram; and sometimes they are not the most appropriate method of teaching points of pronunciation.

Mid plane

The first major limitation is that the commonest type of head diagram shows the mid plane of the head. It therefore shows nothing of the sides of the mouth, which are the most important part in the articulation of certain English sounds.

Such head diagrams are not helpful for describing lateral sounds. The only lateral sound in English is [l]. For this, the tongue-tip touches the alveolar ridge in the centre of the mouth. However, the sides of the tongue are not in contact, allowing the air to escape over the sides. The normal sagittal section is incapable of showing this, and for this reason, the configuration for [l] looks identical to that of [d]. Instead, what is required is a coronal diagram, such as the following (from Brown, 1989), which shows clearly the central contact and lateral passage of air for [l]. Contrast this with the configuration for [ɹ], which is often confused with [l] by learners, but which has exactly the opposite pattern of contact (lateral contact, central passage of air).

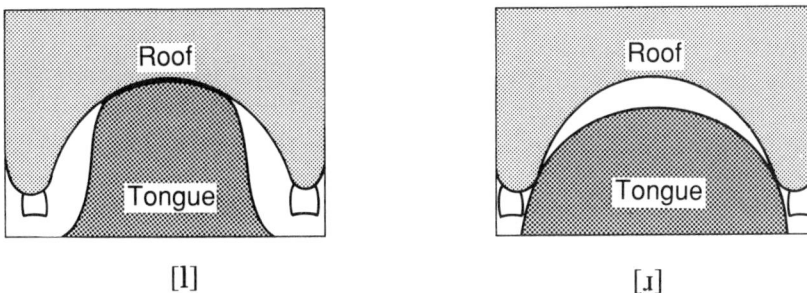

[l] [ɹ]

Figure 2   Coronal sections for [l, ɹ] (from Brown, 1989:296) (by permission of Oxford University Press)

A further point is that since we have two sides to our mouths, lateral sounds may be made on both sides of the mouth (*bilaterally*) or on only one or the other (*unilaterally*). This choice is open for the sound [l], although for almost all speakers, it is made bilaterally. Catford (1988:41) claims that the Welsh sound [ɬ] as in *Llangollen* is normally made unilaterally.

The main difference pointed out in textbooks between the English sounds [s] and [θ] is the place of articulation: [s] is alveolar (tongue-tip or blade against the alveolar ridge) while [θ] is dental (tongue-tip against the upper teeth). However there is a second difference which few books mention (Wells and Colson, 1971:87). This relates to the shape of the tongue. For [s], there is a distinct groove down the centre of the tongue, while for [θ], the tongue has no groove but is flatter (see Figure 3). [s] is therefore known as a *groove* fricative, and [θ] as a *slit* fricative. Note that it is possible to make a dental groove fricative (symbol [s̪]); this sounds like a lisping [s], and gives the impression of effeminacy in British culture. The important point here is that it sounds distinct from both [s] and [θ]. The sagittal section diagram cannot capture this difference; the coronal diagram can.

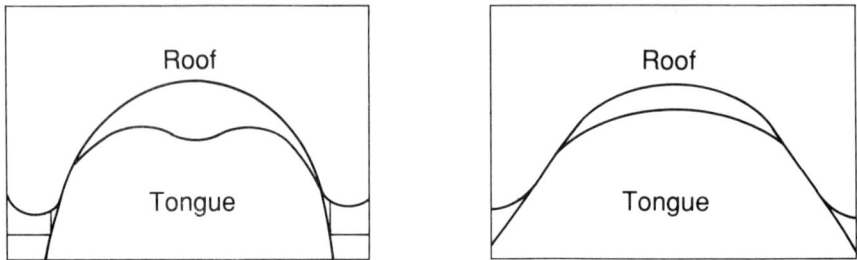

Figure 3   Coronal sections for [s, θ]

The lips can move in a number of dimensions, governed by their musculature. Laver (1980:35ff.) distinguishes three dimensions: horizontal, vertical and protrusion. Of these three, sagittal sections can only capture protrusion. They cannot handle rounding (e.g. for [uː]) and spreading (e.g. for [iː]), which are both combinations of the horizontal and vertical dimensions.

Catford (1988:150) claims that the vowels [uː] (as in English *two*) and [y] (as in French *tu* 'you') normally involve different kinds of lip-rounding. For [uː], there is lip-rounding (i.e. a construction in the horizontal and vertical dimensions) accompanied by lip-protrusion. For [y], on the other hand, there is rounding without protrusion. He refers to these as *inner* and *outer* rounding of the lips respectively. Only the former can be represented on a sagittal section.

Although lip-rounding is of obvious importance in the articulation of several English vowels, it is also required for the [w] consonant. For many English speakers, a fair degree of lip-rounding is also a secondary feature of the articulation of [ɹ, ʃ, ʒ, tʃ, dʒ].

It is clear then that the lips can move in various ways, but that most of these cannot be captured in sagittal sections. It is a pity that textbooks have stopped the practice adopted by Daniel Jones of including 'coronal' pictures of the different possible lip positions. The following line drawings come from his *The Pronunciation of English* (1956). In *An Outline of English Phonetics* (1964), he used photographs of his lips (complete with his moustache) for the same purpose (see also Hooke and Rowell, 1982). In class, a much simpler way of conveying lip positions is simply to make the sound, since the lips are so visible, and to encourage the students to use mirrors to check their own lip-shapes.

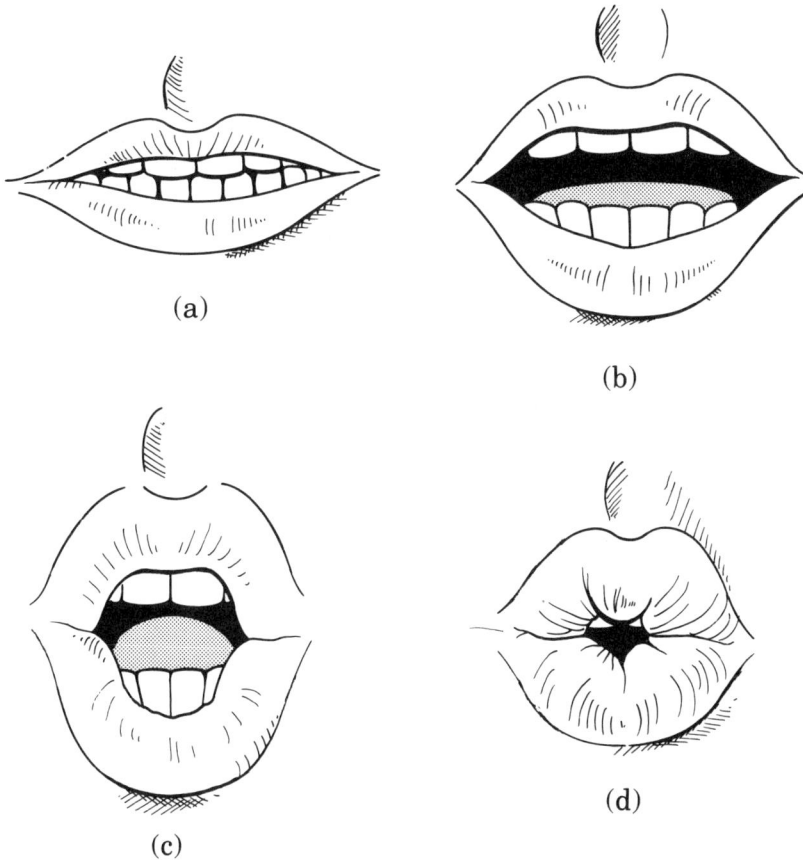

(a)

(b)

(c)

(d)

Figure 4 Types of lip-rounding: (a) Close lip-spreading; (b) Neutral lip position; (c) Open lip-rounding; (d) Close lip-rounding (from Jones, 1956:17) (by permission of Cambridge University Press)

A further limitation of the fact that sagittal sections show the mid plane of the face is that such diagrams are incapable of showing the vocal cords. These are two large flaps of skin and muscle which lie either side of the windpipe. In gestures such as those for a glottal stop or for voicing, the two cords come together along the mid plane (and vibrate for voicing). This means that, strictly speaking, there is nothing to show for the vocal cords in a sagittal section. They must therefore be represented in some diagrammatic way, for instance by using a wavy line for voicing, and one or two straight lines for voicelessness (as in Figure 6 below).

A *static view of speech*

Head diagrams are normally static, in that what they show represents the position of the vocal organs at one point in time. However, speech is not composed of such static positions, in three respects.

Firstly there are certain sounds which are composed of distinguishable parts. That is, they involve movement of the vocal organs. One commonly quoted example is the sound [tʃ], as in *chip*. This sound is in fact a combination of two sounds – a complete closure, and a fricative release. The complete closure is therefore a stop articulation, in that the air is completely blocked from escaping through the mouth for a moment. It is this initial stop articulation which distinguishes [tʃ] from [ʃ], as in *ship*. However, unlike normal stops, like [p], this closure is not released sharply, but slowly, so that the articulators go through a short period of fricative articulation, with an audible hiss (*friction*). This is reflected in the phonetic symbol [tʃ], which is a combination of a stop symbol [t], and a fricative symbol [ʃ].

It must be emphasised that there is more to it than saying that a [tʃ] is composed of a [t] plus a [ʃ]. For example, the [t] in a [tʃ] articulation is not alveolar, but further back in the mouth. Similarly, the [tʃ] articulation does not function as two sounds, but as a single phoneme. So, *why choose* is not identical in pronunciation to *white shoes* (see e.g. Gimson, 1980:172ff.).

Secondly, there are certain sounds which by their very nature are dynamic. For instance, the trill [r], a common stereotype of the Scottish *r*, is produced in the following manner. The tongue-tip is drawn up towards the alveolar ridge. It does not touch it, but is held at such a distance from it, and at such a muscular tension, that the air passing over it causes it to vibrate against the ridge. In other words, this sound can be thought of as being composed of alternate states of closure and opening. For this reason, some writers (Gimson, 1980:35) refer to this as *intermittent closure*.

Neither of the above articulations can be adequately captured in sagittal section diagrams, unless some extra means of representing movement can be devised.

Thirdly, an approach to the description of speech based on sagittal sections often leads readers to think of speech in a static way. However, instrumental analysis has shown that speech is not a succession of postures linked by rapid transitions. Instead, one sound affects, and is affected by, the surrounding sounds, and there are several features which extend over whole stretches of sounds. For instance, the word *morning* contains three nasal sounds – [m], [n] and [ŋ]. For these nasal sounds, the soft palate (*velum*) is lowered, allowing air to escape through the nose, which gives the sounds their characteristic nasal quality. Normally, vowels in English are not nasalised to any appreciable extent. However, the two vowels in the word *morning* are surrounded by nasal sounds, requiring a lowered velum, and so it is not surprising that the velum remains lowered during the production of these vowels too. In technical terms, the vowels have become nasalised because of the surrounding nasals, a kind of assimilation.

Head diagrams showing articulatory positions of the five sounds in the word *morning* are not the best way to emphasise this dynamic nature of speech. Tench (1978) has discussed the dynamic parametric view of speech, showing that a graphic representation of parameters (such as nasality) through time is an effective way of demonstrating the non-static nature of speech.

Airflow

Another very important aspect of speech production is the airstream. For all English speech sounds, the airstream is initiated by the lungs (*pulmonic*) and travels outwards (*egressive*). However, since the airstream is not visible, it is impossible to include it in a head diagram, except by using some convention. A commonly used convention for this is to draw lines with arrowheads to represent the direction of airflow. This works fine for approximants, such as [w], and nasals, such as [m]. However, further complications arise with fricatives and stops.

For fricatives, we need to be able to show that friction is generated, and where in the mouth it is generated. Again, a convention is often used, such as making the line representing airflow wavy in those places where friction is caused.

For stops, the problem is that by definition there is no airflow. For [p], the two lips come together and completely block the air from escaping through the mouth. The velum is also shut, so that no air escapes through the nose either. What we need to be able to show, therefore, is not airflow so much as pressure – pressure which is released when the two lips are released. Technically speaking, pressure is caused in the same way as airflow – by creating a positive air pressure in the vocal apparatus by compressing the lungs. For this reason, books often show pressure by lines with arrowheads (as for airflow), although some readers may find this misleading.

Tongue contact

Strevens (1974), quoted above, states that the sophisticated, intellectualised approach to pronunciation teaching, employing (perhaps graphic) description of articulatory positions, is more likely to succeed for adult learners than for children. It can also be argued that this intellectualised approach is more likely to succeed for consonant sounds rather than vowels. The reason for this is that consonant sounds, by definition, involve a fair amount of contact between articulators, which may form a considerable obstruction to the airstream.

Palatograms are especially useful for showing contact between articulators. Direct palatograms are made in the following way:

1   The roof of the mouth is sprayed with a mixture of charcoal and drinking chocolate.
2   The subject pronounces the sound or word.
3   A mirror is inserted into the mouth at 45°, and a photograph taken.

Where the (wet) tongue touches the roof of the mouth, it removes the powder; untouched areas remain covered in the black powder. The patterns of contact can easily be seen.

Alternatively, a false acrylic palate is made and inserted into the mouth. Otherwise the procedure is the same, except that the palate can be removed for closer examination. False palates therefore allow investigation into the three-dimensional aspects of the articulation, in contrast to the two-dimensional photographs produced in direct palatography. The following palatograms are from Jones (1964) and clearly show the difference between the lateral [l], and the stop [t] (whose palatogram is identical to that of [d]).

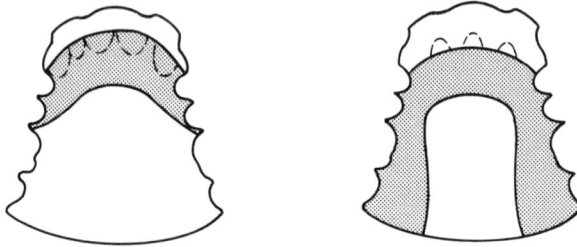

Figure 5   Palatograms for [l, t] (from Jones, 1964:143, 175) (by permission of Cambridge University Press)

In contrast, vowels are produced with little obstruction to the airstream, and consequently little contact between the articulators. The amount of contact involved in vowel articulations tends to depend on the height of the vowel. For high vowels, such as [iː] and [uː], one can feel some contact between the sides of the tongue and the side teeth and gums. However, for low vowels such as [æ] and [ɑː], there is hardly any contact at all between the tongue and the roof and sides of the mouth.

Contact is a very important pedagogical tool, in that it is something which learners can easily feel. It is therefore very difficult for teachers to tell students how to position their tongues in order to make vowel sounds. It is much more sensible for the teacher to rely more heavily on the 'innocence' mimicry approach. Model vowel sounds are pronounced for the learner to imitate and to assess his/her own performance against, perhaps with the help of tape recorders. Sagittal section diagrams are unlikely to do anything other than confuse.

There are certain types of vowel which are impossible to represent in sagittal section diagrams, namely diphthongs. These are vowels, like the [aʊ] of *cow*, where the tongue and/or lips change position, and consequently the sound of the vowel changes during its production. As we have said above, diagrams are inherently static, and are therefore inappropriate for diphthongs, as for consonants like [tʃ, r].

An OHP version of the sagittal section

Figure 6 gives the plans for constructing a movable sagittal section for use on an OHP.

The base is part A. This is best produced on an OHT with a cardboard surround, for greater rigidity. The diagram of part A printed here can be enlarged on a photocopier, using the scale as a rough guide to the eventual size. The other parts must of course be enlarged by the same degree. Once the lines have been traced onto the OHT, they can be drawn over using a permanent marker. The shaded portion of part A may be covered with cardboard, for both rigidity and opacity when projected.

Parts B and F are cut out of OHT plastic. The shaded parts of B, and the whole of parts C, D and E, are made of cardboard. All the movable parts B–F are attached to A by means of wing clips at the punched holes marked 1–5. These points all fall within the shaded, cardboard areas, and the clips will therefore not show on the screen.

The most sophisticated part of the vocal apparatus, and therefore the most difficult to model, is the tongue. For this I suggest a rubber band 18cm in length. This should be cut in such a way that a fold occurs where the tongue-tip is situated. It is then attached with strong glue to point 6 on part B and point 7 on part A. A flexible curve, as used in technical drawing, is generally unsatisfactory as it is not flexible enough.

This OHP version of the sagittal section is cheap, easy to produce and physiologically accurate (with the exception of the diagrammatic representation of the vocal cords). With practice, an adequate level of dexterity can be achieved by the teacher for showing vocal tract configurations on the screen.

References

Baker, A. (1981) *Ship or Sheep? An Intermediate Pronunciation Course* Cambridge University Press.

Brown, A. (1989) 'Giving your students [l/ *ELT Journal* 43:294–301.

Brown, A. (ed., 1991) *Teaching English Pronunciation: A Book of Readings* Routledge, London.

Cant, J.P.N. (1976) 'Phonetic information and pronunciation: some theoretical considerations' *International Review of Applied Linguistics* 14:298–303.

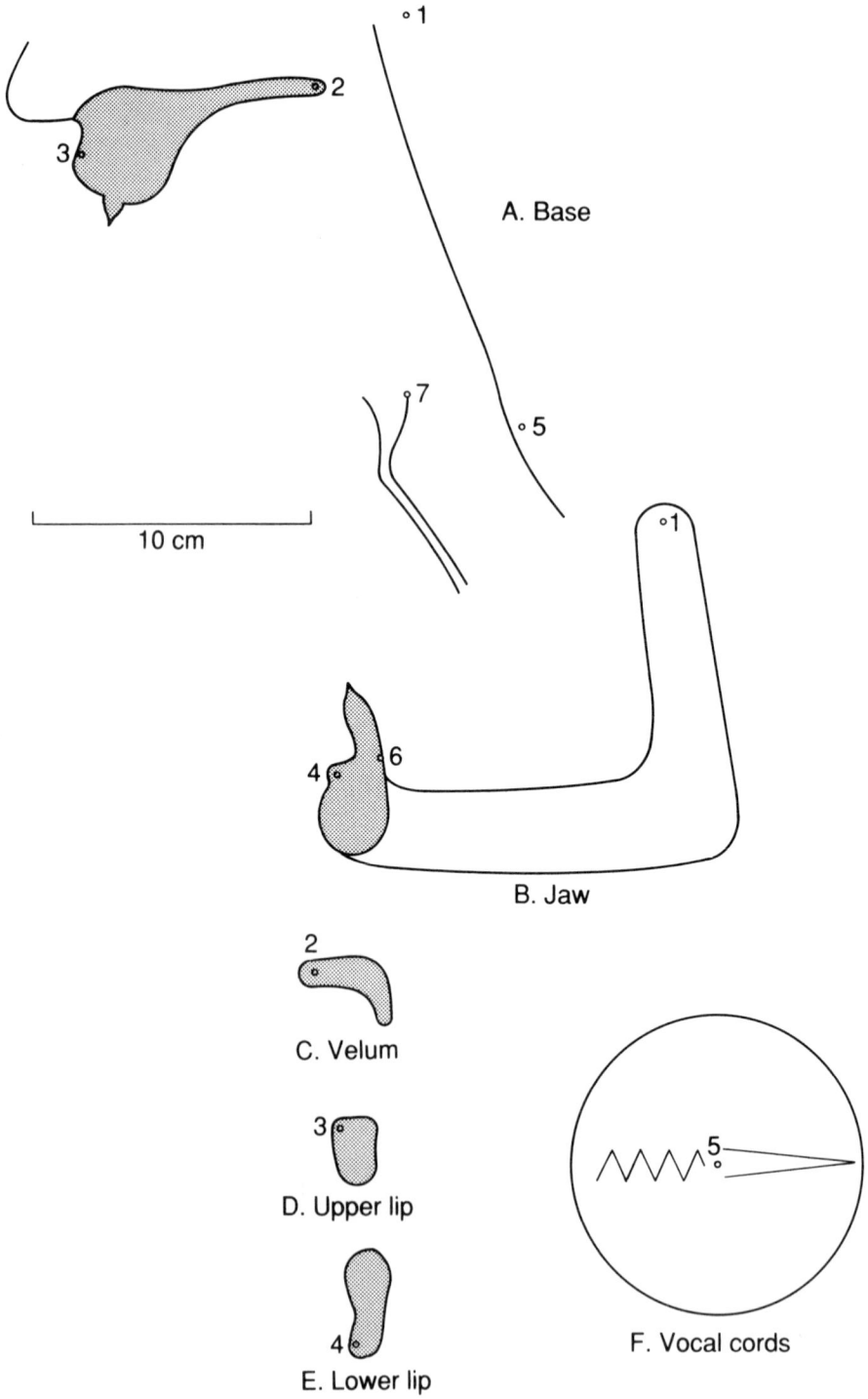

Figure 6 An OHP version of the sagittal section

Catford, J.C. (1988) *A Practical Introduction to Phonetics* Oxford University Press.

Fromkin, V. and Rodman, R. (1978) *An Introduction to Language* (2nd edition) Holt, Rinehart & Winston, New York.

Gilbert, J.B. (1978) 'Gadgets: non-verbal tools for teaching pronunciation' *CATESOL Occasional Papers* 4:68–78. Also in Brown, (ed., 1991), pp. 308–322.

Gimson, A.C. (1980) *An Introduction to the Pronunciation of English* Edward Arnold, London.

Hooke, R. and Rowell, J. (1982) *A Handbook of English Pronunciation* Edward Arnold, London.

Jerome, J.K. (1900) *Three Men on the Bummel* Penguin, 1983.

Jones, D. (1956) *The Pronunciation of English* (4th edition) Cambridge University Press.

Jones, D. (1964) *An Outline of English Phonetics* (9th edition) Heffer, Cambridge.

Kenworthy, J. (1987) *Teaching English Pronunciation* Longman, Harlow.

Ladefoged, P. (1982) *A Course in Phonetics* (2nd edition) Harcourt Brace Jovanovich, New York.

Laver, J. (1980) *The Phonetic Description of Voice Quality* Cambridge University Press.

Strevens, P. (1974) 'A rationale for teaching pronunciation: the rival virtues of innocence and sophistication' *ELT Journal* 28:182–189. Also in A. Brown (ed., 1991), pp. 96–103.

Tench, P. (1978) 'On introducing parametric phonetics' *Journal of the International Phonetic Association* 8:34–43.

Wells, J.C. and Colson, G. (1971) *Practical Phonetics* Pitman, London.

Chapter 12
Visual Displays Develop Awareness of Intelligible Pronunciation Patterns

Garry Molholt
West Chester University

Background: the problem

In a discussion of phonological fossilisation, Elaine Tarone (1987:233) notes that:

> An issue of primary psychological interest is the question of why it is that pronunciation often remains problematic even for advanced learners of the second language (Scovel, 1969). Indeed, adult learners often report that matters of 'accent' may continue to mark them as non-native speakers long after fine points of syntax, semantics, or even style have been mastered. What is the cause of this phenomenal 'fossilisation' of phonology?

One cause of fossilisation is a lack of awareness. The learner does not know the extent to which attempted patterns fit with acceptable patterns. Traditional means of communication do not solve this problem. They give the burden of pattern recognition to the unaware student, and expect the student to perform well in listen-and-repeat exercises. As Bowen *et al.* (1985:145) note, however:

> it is a rare student who can evaluate his own production, who can be his own judge, to determine if a pronunciation is acceptable.

Yet Neufeld (1987:191) suggests that students should tape themselves in order to improve their pronunciation. Then she says:

> Practice and practice, and when you feel that you can pronounce the words properly, re-tape yourself and compare your first tape with your latest version to see how much you have improved.

This approach does not provide learners with a practical way to judge whether or not members of the intended audience will agree that their pronunciation is acceptable. It fails specifically to address the issue of the relationship between actual patterns produced by the learner and required patterns within the range of intelligibility. It may work better with children, however.

In the author's experience, a new approach exists which helps adult learners of a second language to recapture significant aspects of the phonological flexibility lost after their childhood. It involves the insertion of a preliminary step into traditional teaching practices, so that learners are clearly aware of the features they are asked to listen to and repeat. The new aspect is the use of relatively simple and inexpensive real-time visual displays of pronunciation patterns. With a clear characterisation of the closeness of fit between actual and desired patterns, and precise monitoring of progress, the age gap is reduced, so that most adults are able to improve quickly, bringing any of the phonological patterns of their second language well within the ranges of intelligibility. Thus, it seems that fossilisation is more of a problem of pedagogy than of innate ability (Acton, 1984). Multi-sensory communication relating audio signals, visual images, and the physical feelings within the vocal tract provides adult students with the necessary and sufficient information to improve.

The purpose of this chapter is to document specific typical examples of fossilisation of segmental and suprasegmental features which were treated in two minutes or less using a Visi-Pitch 6095/6097 connected to an IBM PS 2 Model 25 personal computer. The Visi-Pitch is relatively small (40 × 18 × 9cm) and inexpensive (under US$3,000). It is available from Kay Elemetrics, 12 Maple Avenue, Pine Brook, New Jersey 07058–9798. Treatment here means that the learner was able to produce the patterns correctly and was sufficiently aware of the patterns so that communication between the teacher and student was established, allowing the teacher to refer to the features in question during other activities, such as conversation, role playing, or presentations. This is seen as a crucial step between fossilisation and self-correction, because of the short time necessary to raise the learner's consciousness, and the ease with which the teacher could then successfully use a more traditional listen-and-repeat approach. It seems to fill an important gap between the learner's perception and traditional methods of teaching, without requiring complex discussions of the linguistic terminology associated with places and manners of articulation. Thus, it does not seem to represent a threat to fluency, a frequent criticism of other approaches to teaching pronunciation.

Three sources of information regarding typical examples of errors are Prator and Robinett (1985), Maddieson (1984), and the author's experience working with over 300 international students and visiting scholars from 1982 to 1990 (Molholt, 1988, 1990). According to Prator and Robinett (1985:xix–xxii):

> Convinced that there are large categories of speech difficulties that all or most of our students have in common, we used a statistical approach to this problem. . . . We recorded the speech, and analyzed and counted the 'errors' of students at UCLA for three years. The result was a sort of frequency count of the pronunciation difficulties of a group of several thousand typical students from abroad. . . . We have adapted an order of arrangement based primarily on simple numerical frequency, consider-

ing first and at greatest length those difficulties most prevalent in our classes.

They present suprasegmental features including stress, rhythm, and intonation before segmental features. Then they include *sandhi*, the euphonic combinations of sounds (linkage) at word and syllable boundaries.

The other statistical approach, Maddieson (1984), provides information on the segmental phonology of 317 language families. From this we are able to determine from a universal standpoint in rank order the extent to which English phonemes are typical. This allows us to predict which phonemes or features in general may be unfamiliar to learners of English. Uncommon features include (*i*) the voicing and loose closure of voiced fricatives; (*ii*) the loose closure of the interdental voiceless fricative /θ/; (*iii*) the voiced affricate /ʤ/; (*iv*) the aspiration of voiceless stops /p, t, k/; and (*v*) lax vowels /ɪ, e, æ, ʊ, ə/.

In the author's experience, the combination of those segmental features of English which from Maddieson (1984) appear uncommon, and those suprasegmental features described by Prator and Robinett (1987), clearly provides a set of topics which needs to be communicated to learners for them to become intelligible. Because of the ease of the multi-sensory approach described here, it is possible to integrate the teaching of segmental and suprasegmental phonology, as needed, rather than to attempt to separate them by teaching one to the exclusion of the other, or teaching one before the other.

The approach advocated in this chapter is that adults are probably able to learn second language phonology as well as children do, in a relatively direct way, using traditional listen-and-repeat exercises, minimal pairs in the contexts of sentences, conversations, and role playing. They need not pay particular attention to complex terminology or notational conventions or differences between categories such as segmental and suprasegmental phonology, as long as they have a quick and easy way to understand the differences between their patterns and the range of desired patterns and to see how well their attempts to change their patterns actually work. The emphasis here is on communication with the learner.

The solution

The 11 graphs presented in this chapter include hundreds of typical patterns and errors according to the sources discussed above. Though they are a very good sample, they are neither intended to be exhaustive nor mutually exclusive. In each case, the learner who produced the error was able to learn in less than two minutes to produce correct patterns and then in subsequent work engage in self-correction or, with a gentle reminder in the listen-and-repeat mode, make the correction.

Thus the learner was judged to be aware of the feature. This contrasts sharply with the many documented cases of so-called fossilisation, including stories of people who maintain a heavy accent even after 40 years or more of living in a country where the new language is used.

Displays

The visual displays include four types of information. As configured for this project, there are two curves.

1   The lower curve shows the *frequency* level of the pitch. This means that the curve for rising intonation will go up and for falling intonation will go down. It also means that voiceless sections will be represented as gaps in the pitch line (since the curve returns to the base line).

2   Above the pitch curve is the *intensity* curve. This second type of information shows the loudness of the acoustic signal. From the intensity curve we can see the relative strengths of the pulses in the rhythm of the speech. Together, the two curves allow us to observe the patterns of stress, intonation, rhythm, voicing, aspiration, closure, turbulence, linkage, addition, deletion, and striation. These are discussed in more detail in relation to the specific displays.

3   A third type of information is provided by the *cursors*. There are two vertical cursors and one horizontal cursor. The vertical cursors (left and right) may be positioned to measure duration. The vertical cursors also provide measurements of the intensity curve, in decibels, and the pitch curve, in Hertz. The figures are given on screen below the displays.

Next is the horizontal cursor. Placed in the upper portion of the display it gives a reference intensity level in decibels. Placed in the lower part of the display it gives a reference pitch level in Hertz. Setting the horizontal cursor in a certain position, the teacher is able to request the students to make only stressed parts of the sentence go above the line or to make pitch go above the line at only appropriate points. This helps students become aware of stress and intonation.

4   The fourth type of information, *statistical* characteristics of the signal, can be provided by the computer, but is beyond the scope of this chapter.

Figures 1 and 2

Figures 1 and 2 provide examples of the visual displays. Both of them show the word *metropolitan*. The first is spoken with normal pronunciation. The un-English second version has stress on the second and fourth syllables (*tro* and *li*), and the three voiceless stops (/t/, /p/ and /t/) are all unaspirated. In both displays, the left and right cursors have been placed to include the vowel between the /p/ and the /l/ in the third syllable.

In Figure 1 we see that the pitch line across the bottom has four parts. This shows that the voicing was broken three times, by the voiceless stops /t/, /p/, and /t/. The pitch line peaks at 147.7Hz, during the /ɒ/ vowel. This vowel has a duration of 0.161 seconds. The aspiration of the voiceless stops /t/, /p/, and /t/ is shown by the small peaks in the intensity curve with no voicing below them.

Figure 2 is quite different. The vowel between /p/ and /l/ is only 0.084 seconds in duration with a maximum pitch of only 111.2Hz. The unaspirated voiceless stops lack the small intensity peaks, and the voicing starts much sooner. Note the difference between the distance from the beginning of the intensity peak of /p/ in Figure 1 to the onset of voicing in the pitch curve, and the shorter distance from the start of the intensity peak of /p/ in Figure 2 to the onset of voicing. The unaspirated voiceless stops in Figure 2 have much shorter voice onset times than the aspirated voiceless stops in Figure 1. Also, the pitch curve in Figure 2 peaks in the second and fourth syllables instead of in the third syllable, and the intensity curves of the second and fourth syllables rise higher than the third syllable.

Thus, we have a clear way of showing the learner differences in patterns. Figures 1 and 2 give examples of stress, rhythm, intonation, voicing, and aspiration. We are able to see the components of stress. As defined by Pennington (1991:135–6):

> Because of the increased energy expended in production, a stressed syllable may be longer, louder, and/or higher in pitch than an unstressed syllable. Thus, the measures of duration, intensity, and frequency are relevant to the description of stress.

It is very common for students to express surprise and even delight when they see their patterns for the first time. Finally they have a way of understanding what well-meaning teachers have been trying to communicate for so long.

Figure 3

Figure 3 is a display of the author's voice saying *twenty years ago*. It is an excerpt taken from a recording of a released form of the Test of Spoken English published by the Educational Testing Service, Princeton, New Jersey. The pitch line is broken only once, for the second /t/. The aspiration of that /t/ is less than the aspiration of the first /t/, which is in word-initial position. The pitch line is unbroken from the second /t/ to the end, because the words are linked and all the sounds are voiced. In this display, the stress is on the word *years*. This can be seen from the peak in pitch, the height of the intensity curve (up to 56.6 decibels), and the duration. For each of the stops (/t/, /t/, and /g/), the energy level of the intensity curve drops to the base line. This corresponds to the slight pause during the build-up of pressure before the explosion of the stop. It is referred to as tight closure. The resulting intensity curve from tight closure has a small peak if the stop is aspirated and a steep slope up to the vowel peak if it is not aspirated. Fricatives, which have loose closure, have different patterns. The /z/ linking *years* and *ago* has a lower energy level than its neighbouring sounds, but it does not drop down to zero. It is also fully voiced, as seen from the pitch curve. Because the initial /j/ of *years* is a glide, there is a slope in the curve as it moves toward the following vowel sound. As can be seen in the following examples of errors, changes in these patterns may result in intelligibility problems.

Figure 4

Figure 4 is from a recording of a speaker of Mandarin Chinese. The left cursor is placed to mark his gap between *twenty* and *years*, and the right cursor marks the stop in *ago*. The pitch is highest for *twenty* and the second syllable of *ago*. The intensity curves are also highest at these points, indicating that stress is on *twenty* and the second syllable of *ago*. The voicing line is broken at three inappropriate places, at the locations of the two cursors and at the end of the word *years*. The second /t/ of *twenty* is missing, so it is not broken there. Since there is a glottal stop at the onset of the word *years*, instead of a glide linking it to *twenty*, *twenty years* sounds like *twenny ears*. The /z/ of *years* and the /g/ of *ago* have become voiceless ([s, k]), as shown by the pitch curve. The entire phrase is spoken in almost monotone pitch with striation (cracking of the voice) at the final vowel. This is shown on the display by scattered dots in the pitch curve.

Figure 5

The speaker of Figure 5 is from Nepal. The entire phrase, *twenty years ago* is included between the left and right cursors. This is very fast. The linkage between *twenty* and *years* does not include a glide at all. The /i:/ of *twenty* is repeated, with slight emphasis, to start the word *years*. There is a large gap in the pitch curve at the link between *years* and *ago*. This shows that the speaker did not voice the /z/, resulting in an [s].

Figure 6

Figure 6 is the author's voice saying *He's tacking the boxes* (from Bowen, 1975:61). The horizontal cursor is placed in the intensity curve so that stressed syllables (the first syllables of *tacking* and *boxes*) appear above the cursor. The pitch also peaks in these syllables.

Figure 7

Figure 7 shows the patterns of a Japanese student saying the same sentence as in Figure 6, *He's tacking the boxes*. The seven syllables here have very little variation in intensity, duration or even voicing. The voicing for each syllable occurs only with the vowels and the nasal. There should only be six syllables. The second syllable is an added *schwa*, which makes the sentence sound like *He's attacking the boxes*. The /z/ of *He's* is voiceless (=[s]). The /t/ of *tacking* is unaspirated. The

/ŋ/ of *tacking* has an added final /k/. The fricative of *the* has tight closure, making it sound like /d/.

This sample was spoken after six attempts at listen-and-repeat exercises to bring out the correct features. This accounts for the slight variation in stress at the appropriate places. Even with faint signals of stress in the correct places, however, without seeing the patterns, the student was unaware of the many other features, including the extra *schwa*, which needed attention before this sentence would be acceptable.

Figures 6 and 7 provide us with an excellent example of a major difference between English and Japanese rhythm. As noted by Pennington (1991:137):

> Languages whose rhythmic properties are based on an alternation of strong (stressed) and weak (unstressed) syllables are termed stressed-timed. English is such a language. In Japanese, the rhythm of the individual syllables making up stretches of speech is relatively regular, which means that there tend not to be major variations in duration from one syllable or phonemic segment (mora) to the next. Thus, Japanese is termed a syllable-timed or mora-timed language (Hoequist, 1983).

She goes on to say that such differences in timing affect linkage across syllable and word boundaries, because the Japanese style is to pronounce relatively even pulses which are not connected.

Figure 8

Another common pattern of the sentence intonation and pitch of Japanese speakers of English is higher stress at or near the beginning of the sentence, quickly and gradually moving down to the end. This is more dramatic than the universal tendency associating decreasing pitch and intensity with utterance finality reported in Pennington (1991:136). In addition to this problem, Figure 8 also displays a lack of appropriate voicing of the /z/ of *He's* and the /b/ of *boxes*.

Figure 9

The nearly monotone pattern of Figure 9 was also produced by a Japanese speaker. Through changes in intensity, he put stress on the syllables *there*, *–ris–* and *south*. The left cursor is located at the voiceless portion of the /p/ of *uprising*. The right cursor is located at the /s/ of *south*. The first break in the pitch curve corresponds to the lack of voicing of the /z/ of *was*. The third break is at the lack of voicing of the /z/ of *uprising*. In fact, this is not a good fricative linking the syllables, since it drops too sharply.

Figure 10

Figure 10 is the same sentence spoken by a French student. Though this was meant to be a statement, it was spoken with rising intonation at the end, making it sound like a question. Again, the cursors are placed at the /p/ of *uprising* and the /s/ of *south*. The first break in the pitch curve is for the lack of voicing of the /z/ of *was*. Stress is on *was*, the second syllable of *uprising* and on *south*.

Figure 11

The final example, Figure 11, was used to show Japanese students that they do have lively patterns in Japanese which do not conform to the relatively dull patterns of their English. It occurred to the author that perhaps the students were trying to be too careful in their English, thus cutting out certain aspects of expression. This could be considered as a feature of their interlanguage. The question of Figure 11 is asked in Japanese. It is 'What did you do?', transliterated roughly as *Naa niishtee te noo*. Here we do not see the evenly spaced syllables of Figures 7 or 8, nor the steady pitch of Figure 9, nor the dramatic drops of pitch and intensity of Figure 8.

Patterns

Whether students follow patterns established in their native language(s) or build new interlingual patterns as they attempt to speak a new language, they need a way to determine the relationship between their patterns and patterns accepted as intelligible. Real-time visual displays of the features of speech signals bring these patterns to life for the students. They provide specificity to a learning environment which has been bogged down in the subjectivity of well-meaning requests to 'try again', 'listen and repeat', 'correct yourself after you hear your tape', 'say it the way I say it', or 'talk to as many people as possible if you want to improve'. They provide organising principles which allow for communication with students without long and complex instruction in the linguistic terminology associated with phonology. They convince the students that success is possible, thereby raising morale, and they let the students develop a sense of appropriate ranges, so students have the confidence to stop trying to improve once the correct patterns have been matched. Each of the errors in the examples was brought to the attention of the students and corrected within two minutes, showing that the students were made aware of the patterns and were able to control them. This forms a foundation for further lessons in pronunciation.

A typical example of an error in rhythm may be found in Figure 7, in which all the syllables are relatively even. Major problems in intonation occur in Figure 8, in which the pitch drops off dramatically toward the end of the sentence, Figure 9, in which the pitch is too flat, and in Figure 10, which has a rise of pitch at the end similar to question intonation. Important stress problems are included in patterns in Figures 2, 4, 9, and 10. Serious errors of linkage occur in Figures 4, 5, 7, and 9.

In addition to errors in these suprasegmental features, numerous errors in segmental features were pointed out in the examples. Voicing problems occurred in Figures 2, 4, 5, 7, 8, and 9. Aspiration errors occurred in Figures 2, 4, and 7. Problems with closure accounted for some of the discussion of Figures 7, 9 and 10. Addition was a problem in Figure 7, in which a *schwa* was inserted between *He's* and *tacking*, making it sound like *He's attacking*. Deletion occurred in Figure 4, in which the second /t/ of *twenty* is missing. Figure 4 also has an example of striation, cracking of the voice, at the end. This is a matter of voice quality.

Kenworthy (1987) provides excellent lessons for teaching supra-segmental phonology. A machine like the Visi-Pitch can bring life to her concepts, such as the following (Kenworthy, 1987:49):

> Learning to perceive a new sound may in some cases be 'an act of will'. You listen to a bit of the new language and try to hear differences between sounds, but two sounds which your teacher *tells* you are different sound exactly the same to you. You must believe they are different, and more importantly, that sometime in the future you *will* be able to hear the two as separate sounds. If you don't have faith or decide not to bother, then you probably won't make the effort necessary to re-tune.

With real-time displays of speech patterns, the 'act of will' becomes an immediate reality.

For segmental features, the exercises in Bowen (1975), which provide minimal pairs in the context of sentences, convince the students of the need to learn the contrasts. As long as there is a way to work on suprasegmental phonology too, these sentences may be used to show rhythm, stress, intonation, and linkage.

There are many ways to integrate visual displays into lessons on spoken English. One way is to use the machine at the beginning of a course and gradually work away from it as conversations, reports, and role playing activities become more developed. Another way is to let the activities begin first and use the machine as needed. Because of the ease of using the machine and the speed with which the students grasp the significance of the pattern matching, both of these approaches seem to work well.

Acknowledgments

The author wishes to thank Professor Peter Kant for reading a draft of this paper. Also, thanks go to the students in English 589, a graduate seminar on the acquisition of second language phonology.

References

Acton, William (1984) 'Changing fossilized pronunciation' in *TESOL Quarterly* 18:71–85. Also in A. Brown (ed.) (1991) *Teaching English Pronunciation: A Book of Readings* Routledge, London, 120–135.

Bowen, J.D. (1975) *Patterns in English Pronunciation* Newbury House, Rowley, Massachusetts.

Bowen, J.D., Madsen, H. and Hilferty, A. (1985) *TESOL Techniques and Procedures* Newbury House, Rowley, Massachusetts.

Dunkel, P. (ed.) (1991) *Computer-Assisted Language Learning and Testing: Research Issues and Practice* Newbury House Division of Harper/Collins, New York.

Educational Testing Service (1982) *Test of Spoken English: Manual for Score Users* Princeton, New Jersey.

Hoequist, C., Jr. (1983) 'Syllable duration in stress-, syllable- and mora-timed languages' *Phonetica* 40:203–237.

Ioup, G. and Tansomboon, A. (1987) 'The acquisition of tone: A maturational perspective' in Ioup and Weinberger (eds.).

Ioup, G. and Weinberger, S. (eds.) (1987) *Interlanguage phonology: The Acquisition of a Second Language Sound System* Newbury House, Rowley, Massachusetts.

Kay Elemetrics (1990) *User Manual for the Visi-Pitch 6095/6097* Pine Brook, New Jersey.

Kenworthy, J. (1987) *Teaching English pronunciation* Longman, Harlow.

Maddieson, I. (1984) *Patterns of sounds* Cambridge University Press.

Molholt, G. (1988) 'Computer assisted instruction in pronunciation for Chinese speakers of American English' *TESOL Quarterly* 22:91–111.

Molholt, G. (1990) 'Spectrographic Analysis and Patterns in Pronunciation' *Computers and the Humanities* 24:81–92.

Neufeld, J. (1987) *A Handbook for technical communication* Prentice-Hall, Englewood Cliffs, New Jersey.

Pennington, M. (1988) 'Teaching pronunciation from the top down' in Sato (ed.).

Pennington, M. (1991) 'Computer assisted analysis of English dialect and interlanguage prosodics' in Dunkel (ed.).

Prator, C. and Robinett, B. (1985) *Manual of American English Pronunciation (Fourth Edition)* Holt Rinehart & Winston, New York.

Sato, C. (ed.) (1988) *The University of Hawai'i Working Papers in English as a Second Language* University of Hawai'i at Monoa: Department of English as a Second Language.

Scovel, T. (1969) 'Foreign accents, language acquisition, and cerebral dominance' *Language Learning* 19:245–254.

Tarone, E. (1987) 'Some influences on the syllable structure of interlanguage' in Ioup and Weinberger (eds).

Visi-Pitch

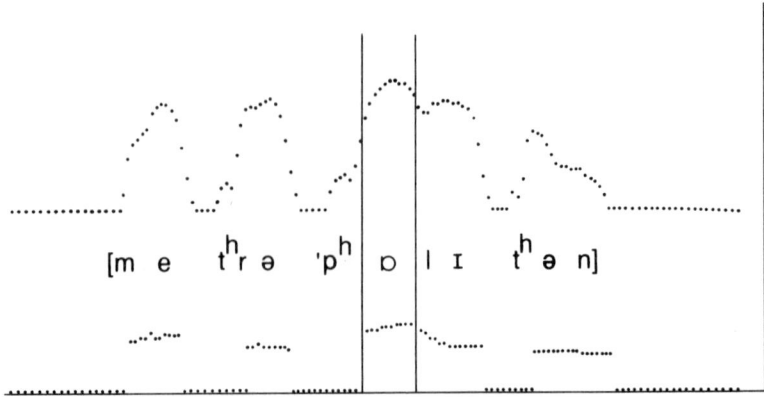

Figure 1   *Metropolitan* (male American speaker)

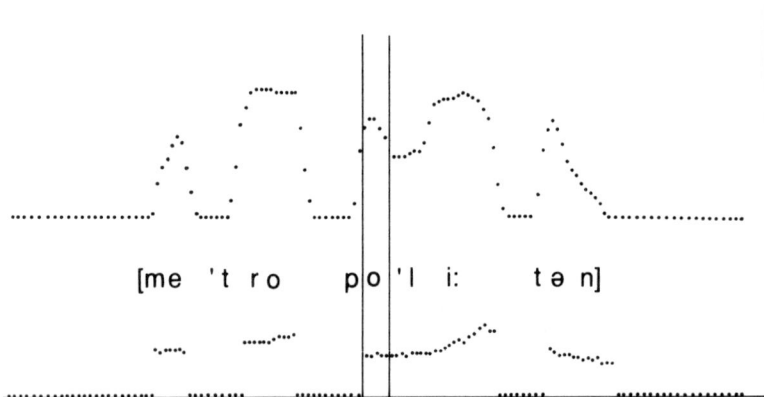

Figure 2   *Metropolitan* (male Bengali speaker)

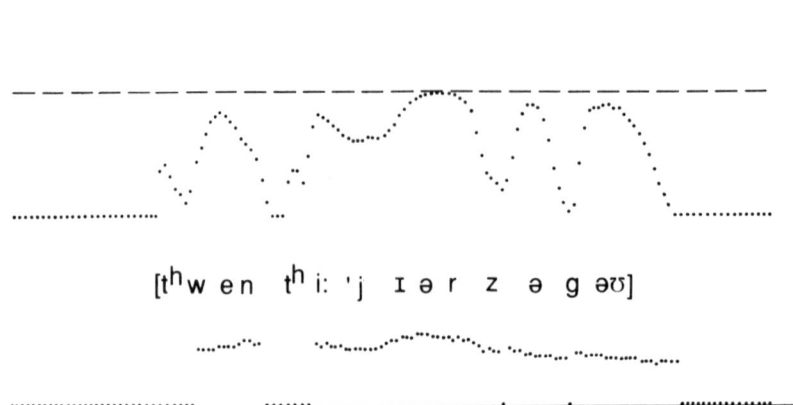

Figure 3   *Twenty years ago* (male American speaker)

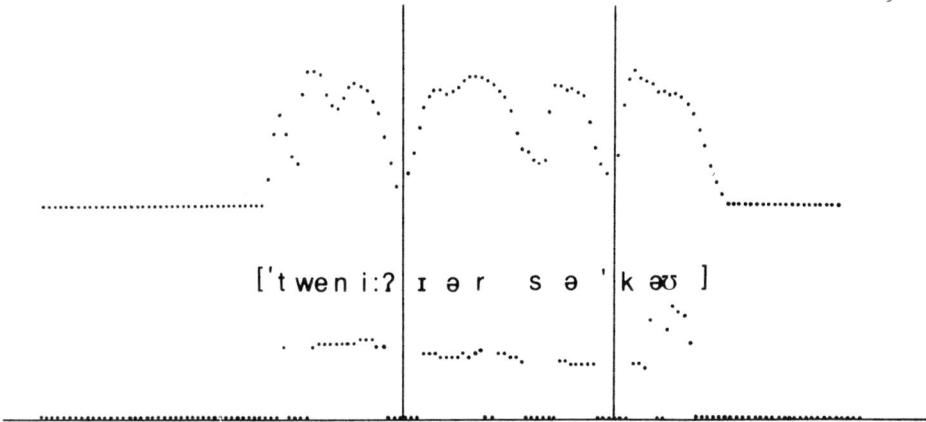

Figure 4   *Twenty years ago* (male Mandarin Chinese speaker)

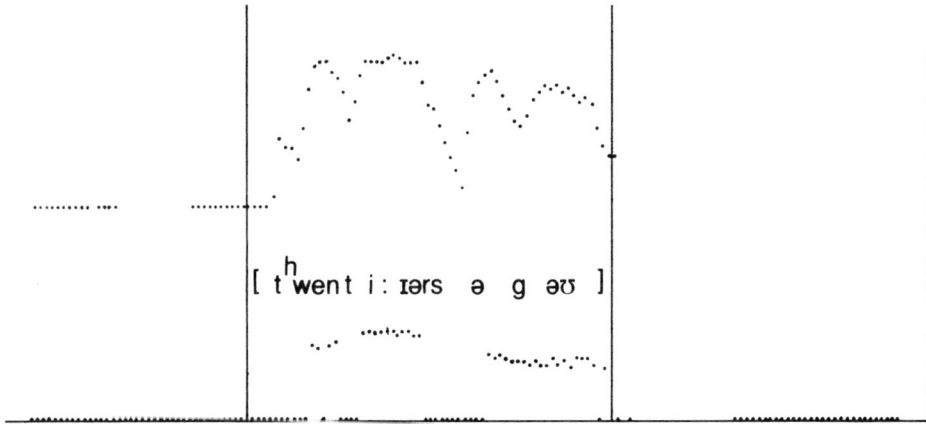

Figure 5   *Twenty years ago* (male Nepalese speaker)

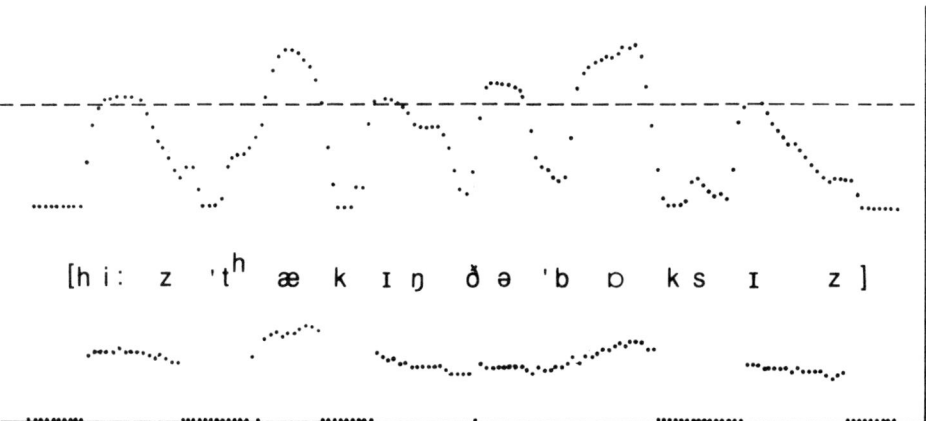

Figure 6   *He's tacking the boxes* (male American speaker)

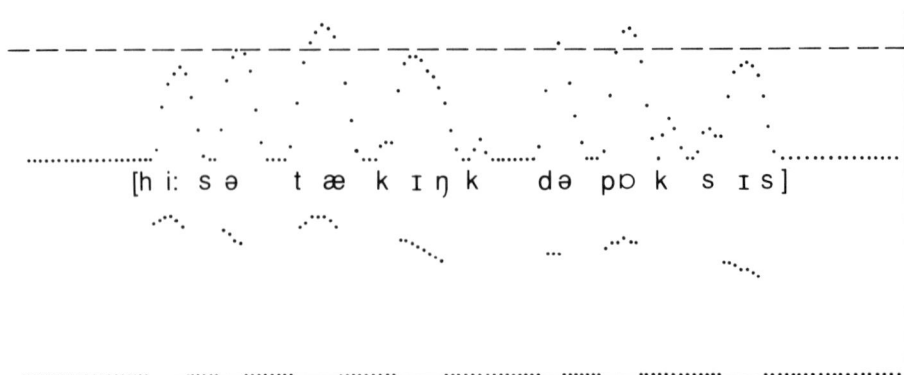

Figure 7   *He's tacking the boxes* (female Japanese speaker)

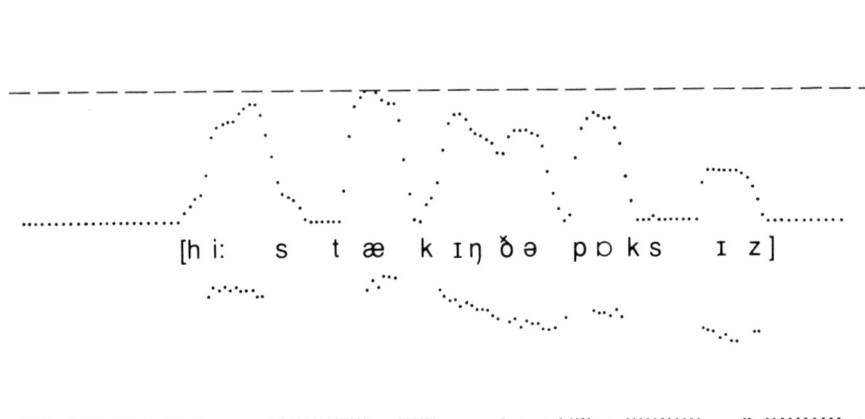

[h iː s ə   t æ k ɪ ŋ k   də pɒ k s ɪ s]

Figure 8   *He's tacking the boxes* (female Japanese speaker)

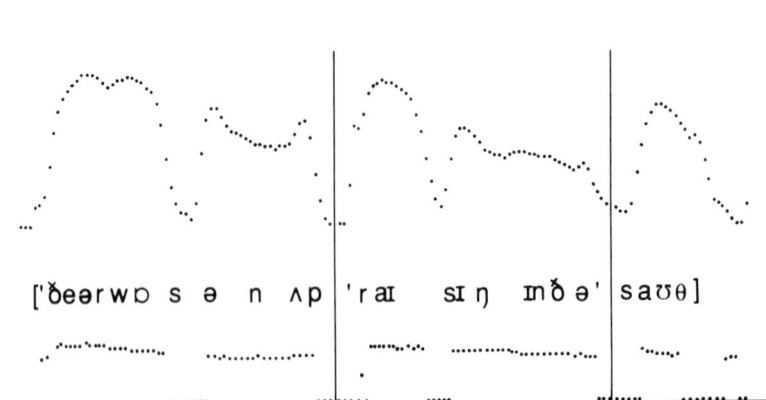

[h iː   s   t æ   k ɪ ŋ ð ə   pɒ k s   ɪ z]

Figure 9   *There was an uprising in the south* (male Japanese speaker)

[ˈðeərwɒ s ə n ʌp ˈraɪ   sɪ ŋ ɪn ð ə ˈ saʊθ]

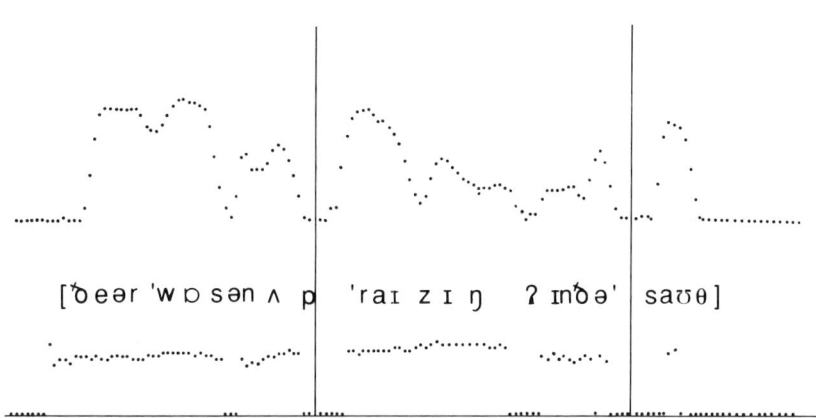

Figure 10   *There was an uprising in the south* (male French speaker)

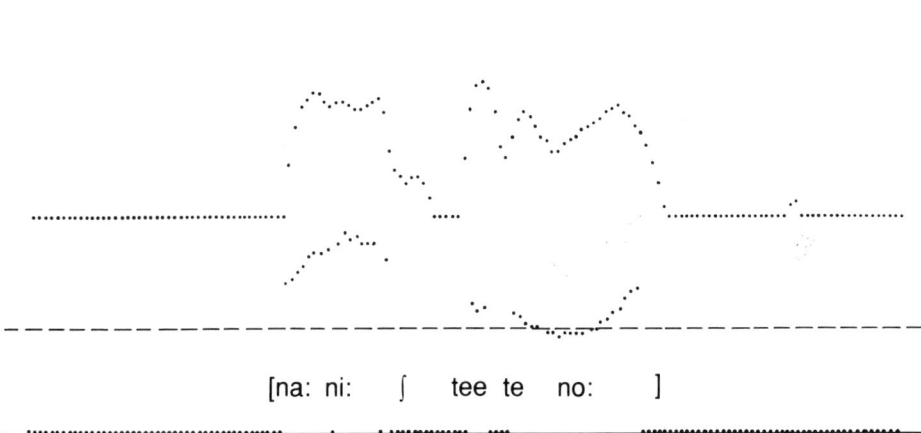

Figure 11   *Naa niishtee te noo* 'What did you do?' (female Japanese speaker)

The Vocal Apparatus

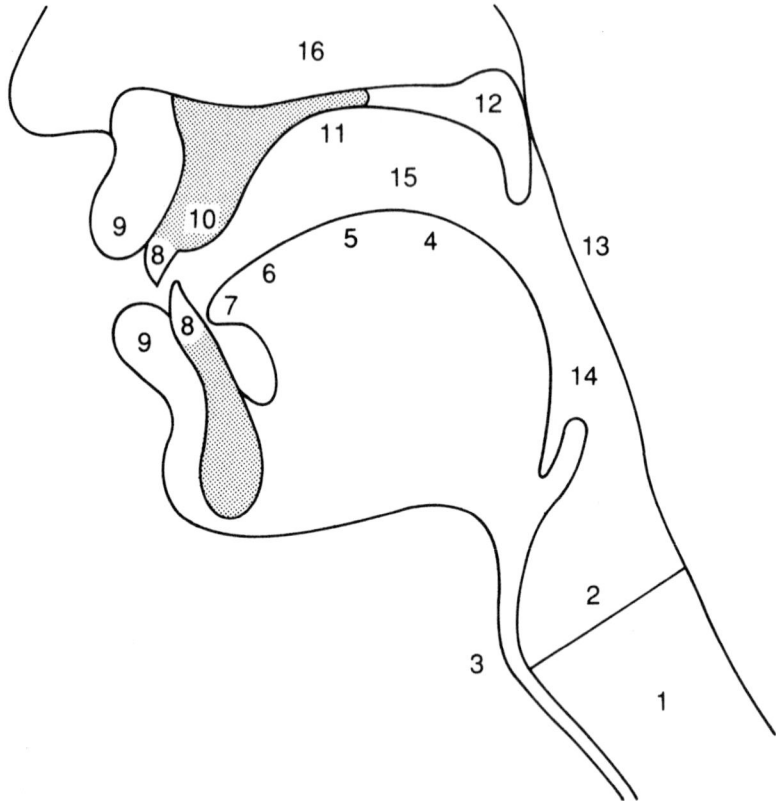

1. Trachea (windpipe)	9. Lips
2. Vocal cords	10. Alveolar ridge
3. Adam's apple	11. Hard palate
4. Tongue back	12. Velum (soft palate)
5. Tongue front	13. Back wall of pharynx
6. Tongue blade	14. Pharyngeal cavity
7. Tongue tip	15. Oral cavity
8. Teeth	16. Nasal cavity

Glossary

This glossary is intended as a guide for teachers to understand the articles in this collection. It is not an exhaustive glossary of technical phonetic terminology. Concepts have therefore also been simplified in some cases.

Accent (i) a person's social, geographical or idiosyncratic style of pronunciation.
    (ii) =word-stress (see *stress*).
Affricate see *manner of articulation*.
Alliteration two words alliterate if they start with the same consonant sound(s), e.g. *stop* and *stare*, *feel* and *phone*.
Allophone a non-distinctive vowel or consonant sound, e.g. the aspirated and unaspirated /k/s of *key* and *ski* are allophones of the same /k/ phonemic unit.
Phonetic **Alphabet** set of phonetic symbols.
Alveolar see *place of articulation*.
Approximant see *manner of articulation*.
Articulation the process of producing a sound with the vocal organs.
Aspiration the burst of voiceless air following the release of certain stop sounds, e.g. the /k/ of *key*. The /k/ of *ski* is, however, unaspirated; there is no burst.
Assimilation a process of simplification which changes speech sounds so that they become similar in certain features to surrounding sounds, e.g. the /t/ of *Great Britain* may change to a /p/ in order to become similar to the following /b/ (thus *Grape Britain*). In coalescent assimilation, two sounds join for similar reasons, e.g. *did you* becomes *didjou*.
Bilabial see *place of articulation*.
Broad see *transcription*.
Catenation see *liaison*.
Cluster two or more consonant sounds occurring in syllable-initial or syllable-final position, e.g. *spots* contains an initial cluster /sp/ and a final cluster /ts/.
Consonant a sound involving a substantial obstruction to the airstream in its articulation.
Coronal section a view of the head, as if you had divided it front from back.
Decibel a unit of loudness, normally plotted on a logarithmic scale.
Dental see *place of articulation*.
Digraph two letters in spelling which represent one sound in pronunciation, e.g. *th* represent /θ/ in *thin*; *ee* represent /iː/ in *see*.
Diphthong a vowel where the tongue and/or lips change position, so that there are two distinguishable parts to the sound, e.g. /aʊ/ in *how*.
Elision a process of simplification, whereby sounds are lost in certain contexts, e.g. the /t/ of *last week* is usually lost in connected speech.
Egressive see *pulmonic*.
Fossilisation a speaker's pronunciation is described as fossilised if, after many years of learning and using the language, the pronunciation is still unsatisfactory, perhaps shows strong features of the speaker's native language, and has reached a plateau in terms of improvement.
Fricative, friction, frictionless see *manner of articulation*.

Functional load the use which a contrast between two phonemes of a language is put to in distinguishing words of the language, e.g. the English vowels /uː/ and /ʊ/ do not distinguish many *minimal pairs* of words, e.g. *pool* and *pull*; they have a low functional load. The frequency of these phonemes in connected speech is also contained in the notion of functional load.

General American a rather vague term describing the pronunciation of perhaps as many as two-thirds of the population of the USA who do not have a recognisably local accent.

Glottal see *place of articulation*.

Groove fricative fricative such as /s/, where the configuration of the tongue involves a groove down the centre.

Hertz (also *cycles per second*) the speed of vibration of the vocal cords during voiced sounds, measured in number of vibrations per second.

Interdental =*dental*, see *place of articulation*.

Intonation the process of using pitch patterns to convey meaning.

Key in intonation, the use of raised or lowered pitch range, in order to show a change of subject, contradiction, etc.

Labio-dental see *place of articulation*.

Lateral see *manner of articulation*.

Liaison the process of linking one word to the next. This involves linking final consonants to initial vowels, e.g. *went up* becomes *wen tup*. Linking /r/ is used in these contexts, e.g. *there* by itself has no /r/ in RP, but an /r/ is introduced for linking purposes in *there are*. Also called *link-up*, *catenation* and *sandhi*.

Link-up see *liaison*.

Loose closure see *manner of articulation*.

Manner of articulation the type of obstruction made for the production of a sound. The following manners are used for English consonant sounds:

Stop (also called *plosive*, and *tight closure* by Molholt, chapter 12): the two articulators come together blocking the air from escaping through the mouth, e.g. /p, d/.

Nasal as for *stops*, except that air escapes through the nose, e.g. /m, n/.

Fricative (also called *loose closure* by Molholt, chapter 12): the active articulator comes towards the passive articulator, so that air escaping between the two makes a hissing noise (called *friction* or *turbulence*), e.g. /f, z/.

Affricate a phonemic unit composed of two parts, a stop articulation followed by a fricative articulation, e.g. /tʃ/.

Approximant (also called *frictionless continuant*): the two articulators come towards each other, but not close enough to cause friction, e.g. /j, w/.

Lateral as for approximants, except that the air escapes at the sides of the mouth, instead of in the centre, e.g. /l/.

Minimal pair two words which differ only in that one word has one sound where the other word has a different sound, e.g. *park* and *bark* are a minimal pair for the /p, b/ sounds.

Monophthong a vowel where the tongue and lips, and therefore the resulting sound, remain more or less constant throughout its production, e.g. /ɑː/ in *calm*.

Monosyllabic having only one syllable, e.g. *buy*, *street* and *look* are monosyllabic words.

Narrow see *transcription*.

Nasal see *manner of articulation*.

Orthography spelling.

Palatal see *place of articulation*.

Palato-alveolar see *place of articulation*.

Phonation see *voice*.

Phoneme a distinctive vowel or consonant unit. RP English has 44 phonemes: 20 vowels and 24 consonants.

Phonetics the study of speech sounds, especially the way they are produced by the vocal organs.

Phonology the study of the way speech sounds are used in a particular language.

Pitch the note of the voice, whether it is high or low. This depends on the speed with which the vocal cords vibrate for voiced sounds.

Pitch range the range from the highest note of a speaker's normal pronunciation to his/her lowest note.

Place of articulation the position in the mouth where a sound is made. This is usually stated in terms of the active articulator (the part of the mouth that moves) and the passive articulator (the part towards which the active articulator moves). The following places are used for English consonant sounds:

	Active articulator	Passive articulator	Examples
Bilabial	Lower lip	Upper lip	/p, b, m, w/
Labio-dental	Lower lip	Upper teeth	/f, v/
Dental	Tongue tip	Upper teeth	/θ, ð/
Alveolar	Tongue tip/blade	Alveolar ridge	/t, d, s, z, n, l/
Post-alveolar	Tongue tip	Rear of alveolar ridge	/r/
Palato-alveolar	Tongue blade/front	Alveolar ridge/palate	/ʃ, ʒ, tʃ, dʒ/
Palatal	Tongue front	Palate	/j/
Velar	Tongue back	Velum	/k, g, ŋ/
Glottal	Two vocal cords		/h/

Plosive see *manner of articulation*.

Post-alveolar see *place of articulation*.

Pulmonic all English speech sounds are *pulmonic* (the lungs create an airstream) and *egressive* (the airstream moves outwards).

Realisation the process of using concrete speech sounds (*allophones*) as manifestations of abstract units (*phonemes*).

Received Pronunciation a social rather than geographical accent of English, often used as a model for learners of British English.

Rhyme two words rhyme if the vowel and any final consonant(s) of the final syllable are the same, or very similar, e.g. *tire* and *higher*, *trade* and *maid*, *right* and *despite*.

Rhythm it is difficult to give a definition for rhythm in language because analysts differ widely in their views. Some say it refers to the occurrence of stresses; others to the incidence of long and short vowels.

Sagittal section a view of the head from the side, as if you had divided it left from right.

Sandhi see *liaison*.

Schwa (also *shwa*) the vowel of the first and last syllables of *performer*. This vowel only occurs in unstressed syllables in English. Also called the *obscure* vowel.

Segmental relating to vowel and consonant sounds.

Simplification the process of simplifying sounds and structures in connected speech, so that they are simpler to pronounce. *Elision, assimilation* and *liaison* are features of simplification.

Slit fricative fricative such as /θ/, where the configuration of the tongue is relatively flat, with no groove.

Stop see *manner of articulation*.

Striation (also *creaky voice*, or *cracking of the voice*) irregular vocal cord vibration heard when a speaker's pitch is very low, i.e. the vocal cords are vibrating very slowly.

Stress Syllables are stressed by being pronounced with one or more of the following features: greater loudness, greater length, a change in pitch. There are at least two uses of stress:

    (i) word-stress (also called word-*accent*), e.g. the difference between an **import** and to im**port**;

    (ii) sentence-stress, e.g. the difference between

        A: 'It's your fault!' B: 'It's **not** my fault.'

        A: 'Who's fault is it?' B: 'It's not **my** fault.'

Strong form see *weak form*.

Supralaryngeal tract the part of the vocal apparatus higher than the larynx, i.e. the pharynx, oral and nasal cavities, and surrounding organs.

Suprasegmental relating to stress, rhythm, intonation and voice quality.

Syllable it is difficult to give a simple definition of the syllable. Suffice it to say that *stress* has one syllable, *English* two, *department* three, and *curriculum* four.

Phonetic **Symbols** marks used to represent sounds in an unambiguous one-to-one relationship.

Tight closure see *manner of articulation*.

Tone (i) (also *tone of voice*) an informal term referring to the use of voice quality, intonation, rhythm etc. to convey meaning.

(ii) in intonation, the major pitch movement in a tone group.

Tone group the basic stretch of speech in intonation, over which a pitch pattern extends.

Transcription the process of using symbols to represent sounds. Transcriptions which show a lot of explicit detail are called **narrow**; those showing little detail are called **broad**. The broadest possible transcription uses only phonemic symbols.

Transverse section a view of the head, as if you had divided it top from bottom.

Triphthong a vowel where the tongue and/or lips change position, so that there are three distinguishable parts to the sound, e.g. /aʊə/ in *tower*.

Unaspirated see *aspiration*.

Unstressed see *stress*.

Velar see *place of articulation*.

Voice vibration of the vocal cords. Sounds produced with this vibration are called **voiced**; those without are **voiceless**. Vocal cord vibration is also called *phonation*.

Voice quality the quasi-permanent setting of a speaker's vocal apparatus, which therefore permeates all his/her vocal output.

Vowel sound where the airstream escapes from the mouth relatively unobstructed.

Weak form the pronunciation of grammatical words (articles, auxiliary verbs, prepositions, conjunctions, etc.) with weak vowels (/ə, ɪ/) and perhaps with simplification, e.g. *must* pronounced /məs/ (weak) rather than /mʌst/ (strong).

Symbols

The following symbols are the commonest set used for the transcription of RP English. They are found in standard textbooks and dictionaries. Other sets of symbols exist, however (see Tench, chapter 8; Dickerson, chapter 9).

Vowels

/iː/	as in *see*	/ɜː/	as in *fur*
/ɪ/	as in *sit*	/ə/	as in *ago*
/e/	as in *ten*	/eɪ/	as in *page*
/æ/	as in *hat*	/əʊ/	as in *home*
/ɑː/	as in *arm*	/aɪ/	as in *five*
/ɒ/	as in *got*	/aʊ/	as in *now*
/ɔː/	as in *saw*	/ɔɪ/	as in *join*
/ʊ/	as in *put*	/ɪə/	as in *near*
/uː/	as in *too*	/eə/	as in *hair*
/ʌ/	as in *cup*	/ʊə/	as in *pure*

Consonants

/p/	as in *pen*	/s/	as in *so*
/b/	as in *bad*	/z/	as in *zoo*
/t/	as in *tea*	/ʃ/	as in *she*
/d/	as in *did*	/ʒ/	as in *vision*
/k/	as in *cat*	/h/	as in *how*
/g/	as in *got*	/m/	as in *man*
/tʃ/	as in *chin*	/n/	as in *no*
/dʒ/	as in *June*	/ŋ/	as in *sing*
/f/	as in *fall*	/l/	as in *leg*
/v/	as in *voice*	/r/	as in *red*
/θ/	as in *thin*	/j/	as in *yes*
/ð/	as in *then*	/w/	as in *wet*

Others

The following symbols are also used in this collection. They are not phonemic units in English. For further explanation, consult a good phonetics book.

[kʰ] voiceless aspirated velar stop
[ɬ] voiceless alveolar lateral-fricative
[r] voiced alveolar trill
[ɹ] voiced post-alveolar approximant
[ʀ] voiced uvular trill
[s̪] voiceless dental groove fricative
[ɾ] voiced alveolar tap
[ʔ] glottal stop
[ʍ] voiceless bilabial approximant
[y] voiced high front rounded vowel

Notes on Contributors

Adam Brown is a Senior Lecturer in the Business Communication Unit of the British Council, Singapore. He has previously taught English and trained teachers at universities in Thailand, Malaysia, Singapore and the UK. His publications include *Teaching English Pronunciation: A Book of Readings* (Routledge, 1991) and *Pronunciation Models* (Singapore University Press, 1991).

Wayne B. Dickerson is Professor of English as an International Language and Linguistics at the University of Illinois at Urbana-Champaign. He has written over 40 journal articles, is the chief editor of *Issues and Developments in English and Applied Linguistics (IDEAL)*, and the author of *Stress in the Speech Stream: The Rhythm of Spoken English* (University of Illinois Press, 1989).

Brita Haycraft is the co-founder, with her husband John, of International House. Her publications include *The Teaching of Pronunciation* (Longman, 1971), *George and Elvira: Conversations in English* (with John Haycraft, Evans, 1972) and *It Depends How You Say It* (with W.R. Lee, Pergamon, 1980). She runs workshops of basic pronunciation exercises, a selection of which will appear in *English Aloud* (Heinemann, forthcoming). She also writes a regular column on pronunciation for the journal *Practical English Teaching*.

Bryan Jenner is a Senior Lecturer in Language Studies at Christ Church College, Canterbury. He was recently Professor of English at Kenyatta University, Nairobi, and a Linguistic Advisor to the Kenyan Commission for Higher Education. He is currently involved in teacher education projects in East Europe and South Africa. He is a member of the editorial panel of the *Journal of the International Phonetic Association*.

Joanne Kenworthy is a Senior Lecturer in English as a Foreign Language and Linguistics at the Polytechnic of East London. She is the author of *Teaching English Pronunciation* (Longman, 1987) and *Language in Action: An Introduction to Modern Linguistics* (Longman, 1991).

Kate Lawrence is a Teaching Fellow at the Institute of Applied Language Studies, University of Edinburgh. She has taught ES/FL in Tanzania, Zimbabwe, Libya and Costa Rica. She is a founder member of *Edinburgh Drama in Language Teaching*, a group formed to promote the use of drama techniques in language teaching. Her interests include the use of literature in the language classroom, especially as a stimulus for fluency work, and the timetabled use of self-access centres.

Jonathan Marks is Regional Teacher Trainer for the Gdansk region under the British Council Polish Access to English (PACE) Programme. He has previously taught at International House in Hastings and Munich. He is the co-author, with Tim Bowen, of a pronunciation resource book for teachers (Longman, forthcoming), and the co-editor of *Speak Out!*, the newsletter of the IATEFL Phonology Special Interest Group.

Garry Molholt is an Assistant Professor of Linguistics and English as a Second Language at West Chester University, Pennsylvania. He is the Co-ordinator of Computer Assisted Instruction for the Department and the Director of the ESL

Institute. He has taught EFL in Saudi Arabia, conducted linguistic research in India, and presented a series of lectures in Taiwan. For five years he was the Co-ordinator of ESL at Rensselaer Polytechnic Institute, Troy, New York.

Lindsay Ross is the Head of Teacher Training at BEET Language Centre, Bournemouth. She has taught ESL and trained teachers in the Strathclyde area, Spain and Mexico. She is the ex-chairperson of the Bournemouth English Language Teachers' Association, and author of *Teaching Tactics: A Handbook for Teachers in Training* (IAMC, Mexico, 1984) and co-author of *Teaching English to Adults in the Strathclyde Area* (Jordanhill Press, 1979).

Paul Tench is a Lecturer in Phonetics and Applied Linguistics at the Centre for Applied English Language Studies, University of Wales, Cardiff. He has travelled widely for the University and the British Council, and was formerly a Senior Lecturer in English Language at the University of Ilorin, Nigeria. He is the author of *Pronunciation Skills* (Macmillan, 1981) and *The Roles of Intonation in English Discourse* (Lang, 1990). He is married, with four children; the family is bilingual in English and Welsh.

Michael Vaughan-Rees currently works for Eurocentres as a teacher, course designer and materials writer. He has taught at schools and universities in Europe and North Africa. He is the founder of the IATEFL Phonology Special Interest Group, and edits its newsletter *Speak Out!* He is the co-author of three books on aspects of social history in Britain during World War II, and has also written a book on London.

Charlyn Wessels is a Senior Lecturer in ELT, and Equal Opportunities Co-ordinator at Stevenson College, Edinburgh. She has taught EFL and trained teachers in Africa, Europe and the UK. She is the author of *Drama* (Oxford University Press, 1987) and a leader of *Edinburgh Drama in Language Teaching*, a teachers' self-help group.